Emotional Regulation

for

Adults with ADHD

Practical Tools and Techniques for
Managing Neurodivergent Challenges to
Improve Your Relationships

Isabella Wells

Dear Reader,

Thank you for choosing "Emotional Regulation for Adults with ADHD". This book is crafted to offer practical tools and techniques for managing the unique challenges of ADHD. My goal is to help you gain better emotional control, enhance your relationships, and improve your overall well-being. I hope these strategies empower you to lead a more balanced and fulfilling life.

Warm regards,

Isabella Wells

Contents

Introduction

Did you know that adults with ADHD experience emotions up to three times more intensely than their neurotypical peers? This heightened emotional sensitivity is not just a side effect of ADHD, but a core feature that profoundly impacts daily life, relationships, and overall well-being.

Welcome to "Emotional Regulation for Adults with ADHD," a comprehensive guide that looks into the complex world of emotions and attention deficit hyperactivity disorder. As a therapist who has dedicated years to understanding and treating ADHD, I've witnessed firsthand the transformative power of effective emotional regulation strategies.

I remember Annabel, a brilliant software engineer who came to my office feeling overwhelmed and on the verge of losing her job. Her ADHD had always made focusing challenging, but it was her emotional outbursts that were jeopardizing her career. In meetings, she would become frustrated with colleagues who couldn't keep up with her rapid-fire ideas, leading to heated arguments and damaged relationships.

Through our work together, Annabel learned to recognize her emotional triggers and developed a toolkit of strategies to manage her reactions. We explored mindfulness techniques, cognitive restructuring, and even incorporated physical exercise into her daily routine. Slowly but surely, Annabel began to regain control of her emotional responses.

One day, about six months into our sessions, Annabel burst into my office with a beaming smile. She had just led a major project presentation without a single emotional hiccup. Her colleagues had praised her clear communication and patience in explaining complex concepts. For Annabel, this wasn't just a professional victory – it was a personal triumph over the emotional turbulence that had defined much of her adult life.

Annabel's story is just one of many I've encountered in my practice, each unique yet bound by the common thread of ADHD-related emotional challenges. These experiences have shown me that with the right tools and understanding, adults with ADHD can not only manage their emotions but harness them as a source of strength and creativity.

In this book, we'll explore the neuroscience behind ADHD and emotional regulation, debunk common myths, and provide practical, evidence-based strategies for managing emotions effectively. We'll delve into topics such as:

- Understanding the ADHD brain and its unique emotional landscape
- Developing a personalized emotional regulation toolkit
- Navigating relationships and workplace challenges

- Embracing neurodiversity while addressing emotional difficulties
- Long-term strategies for maintaining progress and preventing relapse

Whether you're an adult living with ADHD, a loved one seeking to understand and support someone with ADHD, or a professional working in this field, this book offers valuable insights and actionable advice.

Remember, emotional intensity in ADHD isn't a flaw – it's a feature that, when properly channeled, can lead to extraordinary creativity, empathy, and passion. Our goal is not to suppress these emotions but to learn how to ride the waves, turning potential turbulence into a source of power and fulfillment.

Are you ready to embark on this journey of emotional discovery and mastery? Let's dive in and unlock the potential of your ADHD brain!

Chapter One

Understanding ADHD and Emotional Dysregulation

The Neurobiology of ADHD and Emotions

A complicated neurodevelopmental illness, Attention Deficit Hyperactivity illness (ADHD) impacts both adults and children. Problems with attention, impulse control, and emotional regulation are at the heart of attention deficit hyperactivity disorder (ADHD).

Brain areas and neurotransmitter systems that change are hallmarks of attention deficit hyperactivity disorder (ADHD) neurobiology. Attention Deficit/Hyperactivity Disorder (ADHD) is associated with decreased activity and connectivity in the prefrontal cortex, a region of the brain that regulates executive processes like planning, decision-making, and impulse control. Problems with emotional and behavioral regulation may result from this.

When it comes to processing emotions and creating memories, the limbic system—and the amygdala and hippocampus—are indispensable. In ADHD, there may be changes in the size and activation patterns of these structures, contributing to emotional dysregulation and mood swings.

Neurotransmitters, the chemical messengers in the brain, also play a crucial role in ADHD and emotional regulation. Dopamine and norepinephrine are particularly significant, as they are involved in attention, motivation, and mood control. In persons with ADHD, there may be imbalances or inefficiencies in these neurotransmitter systems, leading to difficulties in maintaining emotional stability.

Recent neuroimaging studies have demonstrated that patients with ADHD often have abnormalities in the connection across multiple brain regions, notably in networks involved in emotional regulation. This changed connectivity can result in difficulty in integrating emotional input with cognitive processes, leading to difficulties in emotional self-control and appropriate emotional reactions.

Understanding the neuroscience of ADHD and emotions is critical for designing successful treatment strategies and interventions. It underscores the significance of addressing both cognitive and emotional aspects of the condition and provides a framework for studying specific therapies that can assist improve emotional regulation in individuals with ADHD.

Emotional Dysregulation as a Core ADHD Symptom

While ADHD is frequently linked with inattention, hyperactivity, and impulsivity, emotional dysregulation is increasingly acknowledged as a basic symptom of the illness. Emotional dysregulation refers to difficulty in controlling emotional responses and maintaining emotional stability in the presence of both positive and negative stimuli.

Individuals with ADHD often feel powerful and rapidly fluctuating emotions, which can be tough to regulate. This emotional volatility can emerge in numerous ways, such as:

1. Heightened emotional reactivity: People with ADHD may have higher emotional responses to circumstances that others might find less powerful.

2. Difficulty in emotion identification: Some persons may struggle to appropriately recognize and label their feelings, resulting in confusion and frustration.

3. Impulsive emotional expression: The impulsivity associated with ADHD can extend to emotional outbursts or inappropriate emotional responses.

4. Mood swings: Rapid variations in mood are typical, with individuals feeling rapid transitions from exhilaration to irritation or melancholy.

5. Emotional hyperfocus: Some persons with ADHD may become highly concentrated on a particular emotion, finding it difficult to transfer their attention away from it.

6. Low frustration tolerance: Minor setbacks or hurdles might rise to excessive feelings of annoyance or wrath.

The impact of emotional dysregulation on daily living can be severe. It can influence relationships, work performance, and overall quality of life. Many individuals with ADHD indicate that their emotional struggles are as disruptive, if not more so, than their attentional difficulties.

Recognizing emotional dysregulation as a fundamental symptom of ADHD is critical for several reasons. First, it aids in providing a more comprehensive diagnosis and understanding of the illness. Second, it informs treatment approaches, emphasizing the need for strategies that address both cognitive and emotional elements of ADHD. Finally, it confirms the experiences of many individuals with ADHD who have long struggled with emotional issues but may not have understood them as part of their disease.

Cultural Variations in ADHD and Emotional Expression

ADHD is a neurodevelopmental illness that affects individuals throughout cultures, although its presentation, diagnosis, and management can differ greatly depending on the cultural environment. Understanding these cultural variations is vital for providing culturally appropriate and effective treatment for individuals with ADHD, particularly in the arena of emotional expression and management.

In Western societies, ADHD is generally regarded through a medical lens, with an emphasis on individual symptoms and their influence on personal functioning. However, in many non-Western countries, the concept of ADHD may be less acknowledged or understood differently. For example:

1. Collectivist vs. Individualist Cultures: In collectivist cultures, behaviors associated with ADHD could be viewed more in terms of their impact on community harmony rather than individual achievement. This can alter how emotional dysregulation is perceived and managed.

2. Cultural Norms of Emotional Expressing: Different cultures have varying norms on the appropriate expression of emotions. What might be viewed as emotional dysregulation in one culture could be deemed normal or even desirable in another.

3. Traditional Healing Practices: Some cultures may prefer traditional healing practices or spiritual approaches to manage emotional and behavioral difficulties, rather than Western psychiatric therapies.

4. Educational Systems: The structure and expectations of educational systems vary among

countries, influencing how ADHD-related behaviors are detected and controlled in academic contexts.

5. Gender Roles: Cultural assumptions around gender can dramatically affect how ADHD and emotional dysregulation are seen and managed across various genders.

6. Stigma and Mental Health: The level of stigma associated with mental health issues, particularly ADHD, can vary substantially between cultures, altering diagnosis rates and treatment-seeking behaviors.

Research has demonstrated that there are also cultural disparities in the prevalence and presentation of ADHD symptoms. For instance, some research suggests that hyperactivity-impulsivity symptoms may be less evident in East Asian cultures compared to Western cultures. Still, inattention symptoms may be more constant across cultures.

It's crucial to remember that these cultural variations do not contradict the medical basis of ADHD. Instead, they highlight the intricate interplay between biology, environment, and culture in defining the expression and management of ADHD symptoms, including emotional dysregulation.

Understanding these cultural variances is significant for various reasons:

1. Accurate Diagnosis: Clinicians need to be mindful of cultural differences to avoid misdiagnosis or underdiagnosis of ADHD in varied communities.

2. Effective Treatment: Treatment approaches should be culturally modified to ensure they are acceptable and effective for persons from varied cultural backgrounds.

3. Family Involvement: In many cultures, family plays a key role in health decision-making and support. Understanding cultural norms regarding family dynamics can improve therapy success.

4. Reducing Stigma: Culturally sensitive teaching about ADHD can help reduce stigma and promote acceptance and support for individuals with the disorder.

5. Global Research: Recognizing cultural variations in ADHD presentation might inform more thorough and inclusive research efforts, leading to a better understanding of the illness on a global scale.

In conclusion, whereas ADHD and emotional dysregulation have a neurological base, their expression and management are strongly impacted by cultural variables. A culturally aware approach to diagnosing and treating ADHD is vital for delivering effective, respectful, and inclusive care for individuals across varied cultural backgrounds.

Chapter Two

Foundations of Treatment: Therapy and Medication

Psychotherapy Approaches for Emotional Regulation

Psychotherapy plays a critical role in helping adults with ADHD acquire good emotional control skills. Various therapy approaches have shown promise in addressing the special issues experienced by individuals with ADHD in managing their emotions.

Cognitive Behavioral Therapy (CBT) is one of the most commonly utilized and researched treatment techniques for ADHD. CBT focuses on recognizing and modifying negative thought patterns and actions that contribute to emotional dysregulation. For people with ADHD, CBT can help in understanding emotional triggers, establishing coping mechanisms, and reframing negative self-talk. Techniques such as cognitive restructuring, where individuals learn to challenge and modify problematic thinking, can be particularly good in regulating the high emotions typically experienced by those with ADHD.

Dialectical Behavior Therapy (DBT), initially developed for borderline personality disorder, has been adapted for use with ADHD patients. DBT stresses mindfulness, distress tolerance, emotion regulation, and interpersonal effectiveness. These abilities are particularly significant for persons with ADHD who struggle with impulsivity and emotional reactivity. DBT approaches, such as employing mindfulness to enhance awareness of emotional states and learning to tolerate suffering without acting impulsively, can be helpful tools for emotional regulation.

Acceptance and Commitment Therapy (ACT) is another therapy that can be effective for individuals with ADHD. ACT focuses on accepting thoughts and feelings rather than trying to alter them while committing to activities that accord with personal beliefs. This method can enable individuals with ADHD to build psychological flexibility, lowering the impact of negative thoughts and emotions on behavior.

Mindfulness-Based Cognitive Therapy (MBCT) blends aspects of CBT with mindfulness techniques. For individuals with ADHD, who commonly struggle with present-moment awareness, MBCT can be particularly beneficial in improving the ability to monitor thoughts and emotions without instantly reacting to them. This heightened awareness can lead to greater emotional regulation and reduced impulsivity.

Emotion-Focused Therapy (EFT) is a technique that explicitly tackles emotional processes. EFT can enable adults with ADHD to identify, express, and regulate their emotions more successfully. This therapy focuses on enhancing emotional awareness, learning to accept and control powerful emotions, and generating more adaptive emotional responses.

Group therapy can also be a helpful strategy for adults with ADHD. Group settings give possibilities for peer support, shared learning, and practice of social skills. Structured group therapies, such as skills-based groups focused on emotional regulation, can offer practical tools and a supportive setting for adults with ADHD to work on their emotional issues.

Psychoeducation is a critical component of any therapy approach for ADHD. Understanding the neuroscience of ADHD, its impact on emotional processes, and the rationale behind various coping strategies can empower individuals to take an active role in their emotional regulation.

It's crucial to highlight that therapy for emotional regulation in ADHD often needs to be tailored to accommodate ADHD symptoms. This can involve shorter sessions, more frequent breaks, the use of visual aids, and tangible, practical exercises to sustain engagement and focus.

The choice of therapy strategy should be adapted to the individual's personal needs, preferences, and concomitant conditions. Many therapists utilize an integrated approach, incorporating aspects from different treatment modalities to address the complex emotional regulation issues presented by people with ADHD.

Ultimately, the purpose of psychotherapy for emotional regulation in ADHD is to help patients acquire a set of skills and methods that they may implement in their daily lives. With constant practice and help, adults with ADHD can greatly improve their capacity to manage emotions, leading to better relationships, greater work performance, and higher overall quality of life.

Medication Options and Their Impact on Emotions

Medication has a crucial role in the treatment of ADHD in adults, particularly its impact on emotional regulation. While primarily given to address basic ADHD symptoms such as inattention, hyperactivity, and impulsivity, many drugs also have noteworthy impacts on emotional processes.

Stimulant drugs, including methylphenidate (e.g., Ritalin, Concerta) and amphetamines (e.g., Adderall, Vyvanse), are the first-line pharmacological therapy for ADHD. These drugs act by raising levels of dopamine and norepinephrine in the brain, which can increase focus, reduce impulsivity, and enhance executive functioning. In terms of emotional control, many adults with ADHD say that stimulants make them feel more emotionally stable and less reactive. The greater ability to focus and regulate impulses can lead to better emotional self-regulation.

However, the impact of stimulants on emotions can differ. Some individuals may notice a "flattening" of feelings, feeling less emotionally receptive overall. Others might discover that once the prescription wears off, they suffer a transient increase in irritability or mood fluctuations, sometimes referred to as the "rebound effect."

Non-stimulant drugs are another option for treating ADHD. Atomoxetine (Strattera) is a selective norepinephrine reuptake inhibitor that can improve focus and impulsive control. Some research suggests that atomoxetine may have a good impact on emotional regulation, notably in lowering emotional lability and boosting mood stability.

Alpha-2 agonists such as guanfacine (Intuniv) and clonidine (Kapvay) are sometimes given for ADHD, particularly when there are severe concerns with impulsivity or emotional reactivity. These drugs can help reduce hyperactivity and impulsivity and may have a soothing impact that aids with emotional management.

Antidepressants, while not explicitly authorized for ADHD, are sometimes used, especially when ADHD co-occurs with mood problems. Bupropion (Wellbutrin) is a norepinephrine-dopamine reuptake inhibitor that has demonstrated some success in treating ADHD symptoms and can also aid with mood control. Selective serotonin reuptake inhibitors (SSRIs) may be administered to alleviate comorbid anxiety or depression, which can indirectly benefit emotional regulation.

It's crucial to note that the influence of drugs on emotional control might be quite individual. What works well for one individual may not be as successful for another. Additionally, finding the proper drug and dosage frequently takes a process of trial and modification under the advice of a healthcare expert.

The timing of medication can also alter its effect on emotional regulation. For instance, some adults with ADHD find that taking a small dose of stimulant medicine in the evening might help with emotional regulation during family time, while others prefer to have drug-free periods.

Side effects of ADHD drugs can sometimes influence mental well-being. For example, some individuals may report increased anxiety or irritability, especially while starting a new drug or altering dosages. Individuals need to discuss honestly with their healthcare providers about any emotional changes encountered while on medication.

For some individuals with ADHD, a combination of drugs may be essential to fully address both core ADHD symptoms and emotional control concerns. This can involve combining a stimulant with a non-stimulant medicine or adding a mood stabilizer or antidepressant to the therapy plan.

It's also worth mentioning that while medication can be highly useful in controlling ADHD symptoms and improving emotional regulation, it is not a cure-all. Medication works best when paired with psychotherapy, lifestyle changes, and the development of coping strategies.

Lastly, the decision to utilize medication for ADHD and emotional regulation should be determined on an individual basis, considering the person's specific symptoms, concomitant conditions, lifestyle, and personal preferences. Regular follow-ups with healthcare experts are needed to monitor the effectiveness of medicine and make any required adjustments to enhance treatment outcomes.

Integrating Therapy and Medication for Optimal Results

The mix of psychotherapy and medication in the treatment of ADHD and emotional control disorders frequently delivers the most comprehensive and successful results. This integrated strategy, known as multimodal treatment, targets both the neurobiological and psychosocial elements of ADHD, creating a synergistic effect that can lead to considerable gains in emotional regulation and general functioning.

One of the key benefits of merging treatment and medication is that each component can boost the effectiveness of the other. Medication can help ease basic ADHD symptoms, making it simpler for individuals to engage in and benefit from therapy. For instance, greater concentration and reduced impulsivity due to medication might help patients better focus during treatment sessions, retain and apply learning skills, and finish therapeutic homework assignments.

Conversely, treatment can teach the skills and methods essential to maximize the benefits of medicine. While medication can increase neuronal functioning, therapy teaches individuals how to efficiently use this new capacity. For example, cognitive-behavioral therapy can help patients build metacognitive skills to monitor their emotional states and execute regulation measures, which becomes more practical when medication has improved their cognitive control.

The merging of therapy and medicine also allows for a more individualized treatment approach.

Every individual with ADHD has a distinct profile of symptoms, abilities, and challenges. By integrating medication management with therapy, treatment can be tailored to address specific areas of difficulty. For instance, if medicine efficiently treats inattention but emotional reactivity remains a big issue, therapy can focus more intensely on emotional regulation skills.

Another advantage of this integrated strategy is the capacity to manage comorbid conditions more effectively. ADHD sometimes co-occurs with anxiety, sadness, or other mental health conditions that might affect emotional regulation. While medication could target ADHD symptoms and potentially reduce certain parts of comorbid disorders, therapy might provide targeted interventions for these extra issues.

The combination of therapy and medication can also aid in managing pharmaceutical side effects and adjusting dosage. Therapists can assist patients in creating coping mechanisms for any emotional side effects of medication, such as irritation or emotional blunting. They can also help patients track the effects of medication on their emotional regulation, offering vital data to prescribing physicians to fine-tune treatment.

Psychoeducation, an important component of therapy, can promote drug adherence and overall treatment participation. Understanding the nature of ADHD, how medication works, and the function of various therapeutic options can boost motivation and commitment to treatment. This knowledge can also enable patients to be more active participants in their therapy, establishing a sense of control over their health.

The mixing of therapy and medicine promotes a holistic approach to emotional control. While medicine can help control the neurochemical basis of emotional reactivity, therapy gives a platform to investigate the psychological, social, and environmental elements that influence emotional responses. This complete perspective allows for more robust and sustainable improvements in emotional regulation.

Long-term, the combination of therapy and medicine can lead to better outcomes than either treatment alone. Medication can provide relatively fast symptom alleviation, but therapy fosters abilities and insights that continue to grow over time. This combined strategy can lead to more persistent changes in emotional regulation and general functioning.

It's vital to remember that the integration of therapy and medicines necessitates collaboration among mental health providers. Regular communication between the prescribing physician and the therapist ensures that therapy is cohesive and that any modifications in medication or therapeutic approach are done with a complete grasp of the patient's overall progress.

Ultimately, the goal of merging treatment and medication is to help individuals with ADHD achieve optimal emotional control and enhanced quality of life. This combination approach recognizes that ADHD is a complex disorder that benefits from addressing both its neurological roots and its psychosocial consequences. By harnessing the capabilities of both medication and treatment, individuals with ADHD can acquire a comprehensive set of tools to manage their emotions effectively in many life situations.

Chapter Three

Mindfulness and Cognitive Strategies

Mindfulness Techniques Tailored for ADHD Brains

Mindfulness, the practice of focusing one's attention on the present moment without judgment, has gained substantial momentum as an effective solution for those with Attention Deficit Hyperactivity Disorder (ADHD). However, typical mindfulness techniques can prove tough for persons with ADHD due to their inherent challenges with attention and focus. This has led to the creation of specialized mindfulness practices that cater directly to the unique needs and characteristics of ADHD brains.

One major adaptation is the use of shorter, more frequent mindfulness sessions. Instead of extended meditation times, which can be stressful for those with ADHD, brief 2-5 minute practices spaced throughout the day can be more bearable and helpful. These "micro-mindfulness" moments can be introduced into regular routines, such as mindful breathing while waiting in line or exercising body awareness during a short work break.

Another key adjustment is the introduction of movement into mindfulness activities. Given that many individuals with ADHD struggle with sitting still, practices like walking meditation, mindful stretching, or even mindful fidgeting can assist in channeling excess energy while still building present-moment awareness. This method coincides with the natural tendencies of ADHD brains, making it simpler to engage in and maintain mindfulness activities.

Sensory-rich mindfulness activities can also be particularly effective for those with ADHD. Engaging numerous senses simultaneously can help maintain focus and interest. For example, mindful eating techniques that entail gently appreciating the flavor, texture, and fragrance of food can be both engaging and grounded. Similarly, nature-based mindfulness activities that include watching and interacting with the external environment can provide a plethora of sensory information to anchor attention.

The usage of technology and applications can also play a vital part in personalizing mindfulness for ADHD minds. Many individuals with ADHD respond well to visual and aural stimuli, making guided meditation apps or virtual reality mindfulness sessions particularly helpful tools. These technologies can give structured, interactive mindfulness programs that adapt to shorter attention spans and provide quick feedback, which can be motivating for persons with ADHD.

Mindfulness approaches that focus on strengthening emotional regulation are particularly useful for those with ADHD, who typically struggle with emotional impulsivity. Practices like the "STOP" approach (Stop, Take a breath, Observe, Proceed) can be very beneficial in managing emotional reactivity. This strategy encourages a brief stop and moment of awareness before responding to emotional triggers, which can be helpful for persons with ADHD who tend to react rapidly and powerfully to emotional inputs.

Another key part of customizing mindfulness for ADHD brains is the emphasis on self-compassion and non-judgment. Many individuals with ADHD have internalized poor self-perceptions owing to years of battling with attention and impulse control. Mindfulness practices that expressly involve self-compassion can help counterbalance these negative thought patterns and establish a more positive self-image.

It's also important to frame mindfulness activities in terms of their practical advantages for ADHD symptoms. For instance, emphasizing how mindfulness can improve focus, reduce impulsivity, or promote emotional regulation might raise motivation and engagement with the practices. This approach correlates with the tendency of individuals with ADHD to be more interested when they comprehend the immediate relevance and advantages of an activity.

Lastly, incorporating mindfulness into daily activities, rather than considering it as a separate discipline, can be particularly useful for persons with ADHD. This might involve practicing attentive awareness while completing ordinary tasks like brushing teeth, doing dishes, or commuting. By integrating mindfulness into everyday life, it becomes more accessible and durable for individuals who would struggle with sustaining a separate meditation practice.

In conclusion, while standard mindfulness activities might be tough for those with ADHD, personalized approaches that reflect the particular characteristics of ADHD brains can be highly successful. By including exercise, engaging many senses, employing technology, focusing on emotional regulation, emphasizing self-compassion, and integrating mindfulness into daily life, these modified strategies can give considerable benefits in treating ADHD symptoms and enhancing overall well-being.

Cognitive Behavioral Strategies for Emotion Management

Cognitive Behavioral Therapy (CBT) has emerged as a highly effective strategy for managing the emotional problems associated with ADHD. By concentrating on the interplay between thoughts, feelings, and behaviors, CBT provides a systematic framework for individuals with ADHD to better understand and regulate their emotions. This section covers key cognitive behavioral methods customized for emotion control in the context of ADHD.

One essential CBT strategy is cognitive restructuring, which includes identifying and addressing negative thought patterns that contribute to emotional distress. For those with ADHD, who commonly battle with negative self-talk and catastrophizing, this method can be particularly effective. The method often begins with recognizing automatic negative thoughts, such as "I always mess things up" or "I'll never be able to control my emotions." Once discovered, these thoughts are investigated for their validity and reframed in a more balanced and realistic manner.

Another essential method is the usage of thinking logs. This entails meticulously documenting emotional events, including the triggering situations, accompanying thoughts, and resultant emotions and behaviors. For individuals with ADHD, who may have trouble recalling or evaluating their emotional experiences, thought logs give a solid instrument for self-reflection and pattern discovery. Over time, this practice can lead to enhanced emotional self-awareness and the ability to identify repeated triggers and thought patterns.

Behavioral activation is another major component of CBT that can be particularly useful for those with ADHD suffering from mood management. This method involves arranging and engaging in activities that bring a sense of accomplishment or enjoyment, even when motivation is low. For persons with ADHD, who may struggle with initiating tasks or following through on plans, dividing activities into smaller, more manageable steps and using external reminders and rewards might boost the success of this strategy.

Problem-solving skills are also important to CBT and can be used for ADHD-related emotional issues. This involves systematically identifying problems, creating viable solutions, analyzing these possibilities, and implementing and reviewing the chosen solution. For persons with ADHD, who may feel overwhelmed by circumstances or struggle with impulsive decision-making, this structured method can provide a sense of control and enhance emotional regulation in challenging situations.

Mindfulness-based cognitive therapy (MBCT) integrates classic CBT procedures with mindfulness practices, giving a potent strategy for emotion control in ADHD. MBCT helps individuals develop a non-judgmental awareness of their thoughts and emotions, lessening the tendency to become caught up in negative thought spirals. For persons with ADHD, who typically experience rushing thoughts and emotional reactivity, MBCT can provide methods for generating space between thoughts and reactions, allowing for more measured emotional responses.

Exposure treatment, often associated with anxiety disorders, can also be modified for emotion control in ADHD. This entails gradually exposing individuals to circumstances that generate emotional pain while providing them with coping mechanisms. For persons with ADHD who may avoid particular circumstances owing to fear of emotional dysregulation, controlled exposure can help build confidence and establish more adaptive emotional responses over time.

Role-playing and social skills training are helpful CBT tools for treating interpersonal and emotional problems typical of ADHD. These strategies entail rehearsing difficult social circumstances in a controlled environment, allowing individuals to build and perfect their emotional regulation skills in social contexts. This can be particularly advantageous for persons with ADHD who struggle with impulsive communication or understanding social signs.

Self-monitoring is another key CBT strategy for mood control in ADHD. This involves frequently documenting emotional states, triggers, and coping mechanisms. For those with ADHD, who may have difficulties retaining awareness of their emotional patterns, self-monitoring can provide significant insights and a sense of agency in managing their emotions.

Finally, relaxation techniques such as progressive muscle relaxation, deep breathing exercises, and guided imagery are significant components of CBT for emotion control. These activities can assist individuals with ADHD reduce physical tension and arousal, which commonly accompany emotional distress. Regular application of these approaches can lead to greater general emotional regulation and stress management.

In conclusion, cognitive-behavioral methods offer a comprehensive arsenal for emotion control in individuals with ADHD. By addressing both cognitive patterns and behavioral reactions, these techniques provide practical, skills-based approaches to improve emotional control. When customized to the specific issues of ADHD, such as difficulty with focus, impulsivity, and self-awareness, these tactics can greatly boost emotional well-being and overall functioning.

Developing a Growth Mindset for Emotional Challenges

Developing a development mindset is a powerful method for those with ADHD confronting emotional issues. This concept, pioneered by psychologist Carol Dweck, promotes the belief that abilities and intelligence can be developed via effort, learning, and persistence. For persons with

ADHD, who often struggle with emotional control and may have internalized negative views about their skills, adopting a growth mindset can be transformative in managing emotional issues.

At its root, a growth mindset in the context of ADHD and emotional regulation includes reframing obstacles as opportunities for learning and progress rather than fixed constraints. This adjustment in viewpoint can dramatically alter how individuals approach and cope with emotional issues. Instead of perceiving emotional dysregulation as an immutable component of their ADHD, individuals might see it as an area for possible progress and skill development.

One crucial part of having a growth mindset for emotional issues is detecting and addressing fixed mentality notions. For example, sentiments like "I'll always be bad at controlling my emotions" or "There's no point in trying to improve my emotional reactions" reveal a fixed attitude. Individuals with

ADHD can learn to detect these thoughts and consciously replace them with growth-oriented alternatives such as "I'm learning to manage my emotions better every day" or "Each emotional challenge is an opportunity to practice and improve my regulation skills."

Another crucial factor is embracing the process of learning and progress rather than focusing exclusively on outcomes. For those with ADHD, who may have repeated failures in emotional regulation, this adjustment can be particularly beneficial. Celebrating minor changes and efforts made, rather than just "perfect" emotional responses, can help retain motivation and build resilience. This can mean noticing attempts to utilize coping skills, even if they weren't successful, or recognizing progressive increases in emotional awareness over time.

Reframing failure is also vital in creating a development mindset for emotional issues. Instead of viewing emotional outbursts or regulation failures as personal flaws, individuals with ADHD can learn to see them as useful learning experiences. This might involve assessing what prompted the emotional reaction, what solutions were explored, and what could be done differently next time. By tackling emotional obstacles with inquiry rather than self-criticism, individuals can turn setbacks into stepping stones for growth.

Developing a growth mentality also involves practicing self-compassion. Many individuals with ADHD have a severe inner critic, particularly when it comes to emotional regulation. Learning to treat oneself with kindness and understanding, especially amid emotional obstacles, is vital for retaining a growth-oriented viewpoint. This could require practicing self-compassionate self-talk, such as "It's okay to struggle sometimes; I'm doing my best to improve."

Setting realistic and progressive goals is another crucial method in fostering a growth mindset for emotional issues. For those with ADHD, who may feel overwhelmed by the notion of "perfect" emotional control, breaking down emotional regulation into smaller, manageable goals can be immensely motivating. This can involve setting aims like "I will practice deep breathing once a day this week" or "I will identify my emotions before reacting in at least one challenging situation today."

Seeking out and welcoming feedback is also vital in creating a growth attitude. For persons with ADHD, who may have difficulties accurately judging their emotional responses, comments from trustworthy friends, family members, or therapists can provide significant insights for progress. Learning to view constructive criticism as valuable information rather than personal attacks is a crucial ability in keeping a growth-oriented viewpoint.

Modeling and surrounding oneself with growth mindset influencers can also be beneficial. This can mean finding tales of persons who have successfully improved their emotional regulation abilities, joining support groups focused on personal growth, or working with a therapist who emphasizes a growth-oriented approach to ADHD management.

Lastly, having a growth mindset for emotional issues entails acknowledging the significance of effort and strategy in change. Rather than attributing emotional regulation achievements or failures to natural talent or luck, individuals with ADHD can learn to connect their efforts and chosen techniques to outcomes. This underscores the assumption that emotional control abilities may be acquired and perfected over time with committed practice and proper strategies.

In conclusion, establishing a development mindset for emotional issues can be a game-changer for those with ADHD. By reframing obstacles as opportunities for progress, embracing the learning process, practicing self-compassion, setting incremental objectives, receiving feedback, and acknowledging the significance of effort and strategy, individuals can shift their approach to emotional regulation. This perspective adjustment not only improves emotional management abilities but also boosts general resilience, self-efficacy, and well-being in the face of ADHD-related obstacles.

Chapter Four

Building Emotional Intelligence and Resilience

Recognizing and Mapping Personal Emotional Patterns

Recognizing and mapping personal emotional patterns is a vital step in developing emotional intelligence and resilience, particularly for those with ADHD who often experience powerful and rapidly changing emotions. This approach entails obtaining a profound grasp of one's emotional landscape, including triggers, reactions, and habitual responses. By becoming more aware of these patterns, individuals can take proactive actions to manage their emotions more efficiently.

The first step in understanding emotional patterns is gaining emotional literacy. This involves expanding one's vocabulary for describing emotions beyond basic terms like "happy," "sad," or "angry." Individuals with ADHD can benefit from exploring more nuanced emotional terms, such as "frustrated," "overwhelmed," "anxious," or "elated." This expanded emotional vocabulary allows for more precise identification and expression of feelings, which is essential for effective emotional management.

Keeping an emotion journal is a helpful strategy for mapping emotional patterns. This involves frequently recording emotional experiences, including the situation that produced the emotion, the strength of the feeling, bodily sensations linked with the emotion, thoughts that accompanied it, and any ensuing behaviors. Over time, this technique can show recurring patterns and help individuals recognize common triggers and habitual responses.

Another effective strategy is the building of an emotional wheel or map. This visual representation can enable individuals with ADHD, who typically benefit from visual aids, to see the links between different emotions and events. The emotional wheel often places key emotions at the center (e.g., joy, sadness, anger, fear) and branches out to more specific and complex emotions. Users can then tie these emotions to specific triggers or occurrences in their lives.

Tracking emotional trends throughout the day can also be illuminating. Many individuals with ADHD experience swings in emotional states that connect with their daily routines, medication cycles, or external variables like work stress or social interactions. By documenting emotional experiences at different times of the day, patterns may develop that can suggest techniques for emotional regulation.

Identifying emotional triggers is another key component of mapping emotional patterns. Triggers can be external (e.g., certain surroundings, encounters with specific individuals, or types of tasks) or internal (e.g., thoughts, bodily sensations, or memories). For those with ADHD, common triggers could include feeling overwhelmed by tasks, suffering time pressure, or facing unexpected changes in plans. Recognizing these triggers enables the development of proactive coping techniques.

Understanding the connection between emotions and ADHD symptoms is also crucial. For example, emotional dysregulation in ADHD can sometimes be misinterpreted for mood swings or other mood disorders. Recognizing how ADHD symptoms like impulsivity, inattention, or hyperactivity interact with emotional events can provide essential context for understanding one's emotional patterns.

Exploring the strength and duration of emotional responses is another crucial part of mapping emotional patterns. Individuals with ADHD often experience emotions more vividly and may have difficulties managing the length of emotional states. By measuring the intensity and length of different emotions, individuals can acquire insight into which emotions tend to be most problematic to control and build specific strategies for these particular emotional states.

It's also helpful to analyze the cognitive patterns linked with different emotions. This can involve detecting typical thinking distortions or negative self-talk that accompany certain emotional states. For instance, an individual with ADHD might notice a pattern of catastrophizing thoughts when feeling stressed about a deadline.

Lastly, understanding and mapping emotional patterns should include an exploration of coping techniques, both adaptive and maladaptive. This involves analyzing what tactics an individual normally utilizes to control different emotions and evaluating their effectiveness. For example, someone might notice they tend to employ avoidance as a coping method for worry, which provides short-term respite but often exacerbates the problem in the long run.

By engaging in this extensive process of noticing and mapping emotional patterns, individuals with ADHD can acquire vital insights into their emotional experiences. This self-knowledge forms the foundation for establishing more effective emotional regulation tools, boosting self-awareness, and building general emotional intelligence and resilience.

Enhancing Self-Awareness and Empathy

Enhancing self-awareness and empathy is a vital component of improving emotional intelligence and resilience, particularly for those with ADHD who may struggle with emotional regulation and social relationships. Self-awareness entails a thorough grasp of one's own emotions, thoughts, and behaviors, whereas empathy is the ability to comprehend and share the experiences of others. Developing these skills can considerably improve emotional control and interpersonal interactions.

To promote self-awareness, individuals with ADHD can start by practicing regular self-reflection. This might involve setting aside time each day to check in with oneself, asking questions like "How am I feeling right now?" and "What thoughts are going through my mind?" This practice can be particularly beneficial for those with ADHD who may tend to act on impulse without fully processing their internal state.

Mindfulness meditation is another excellent tool for enhancing self-awareness. By focusing attention on the present moment without judgment, individuals can become more attuned to their thoughts, emotions, and body sensations. For persons with ADHD, shorter, more frequent mindfulness exercises or guided meditations could be more doable and helpful than longer, unstructured practices.

Body scan exercises can assist individuals with ADHD become more aware of the physical expressions of their emotions. This entails systematically focusing attention on different sections of the body, noting any sensations or tensions. Over time, this practice can help individuals notice early bodily signals of emotional changes, allowing for more proactive emotional regulation.

Feedback from trusted persons can also play a key role in developing self-awareness. Individuals with

ADHD could have difficulties appropriately perceiving their own behaviors or emotional expressions. Seeking honest, constructive feedback from friends, family, or therapists can provide vital insights into blind spots and places for progress.

Journaling is another helpful approach for enhancing self-awareness. Regular writing about one's experiences, ideas, and feelings might reveal patterns and insights that would not be visible in day-to-day life. For persons with ADHD who might struggle with consistent journaling, adopting prompts or organized journaling applications might assist in maintaining the practice.

Developing empathy generally begins with improved listening skills. Active listening entails completely concentrating on what is being said rather than merely passively receiving the message. For those with ADHD who can have trouble with focus during discussions, using active listening strategies like summarizing what the other person has said or asking clarifying questions can boost understanding and connection.

Perspective-taking exercises can also enhance empathy. This entails picturing circumstances from another person's point of view. For those with ADHD, who might tend to focus on their own experiences, consciously exercising perspective-taking might extend their awareness of others' emotions and motivations.

Reading fiction has been demonstrated to improve empathy by allowing readers to immerse themselves in the thoughts and feelings of characters. For persons with ADHD who might find sustained reading problematic, audiobooks or graphic novels can be intriguing alternatives.

Volunteering or engaging in community service can provide real-world opportunities to develop empathy. These experiences expose individuals to varied perspectives and life situations, promoting a broader awareness of others' experiences and emotions.

Role-playing exercises can be particularly effective for those with ADHD in increasing both self-awareness and empathy. By acting out diverse events, individuals can get insights into their emotional responses and experience seeing things from multiple viewpoints.

Learning to identify and analyze non-verbal cues is another key part of building empathy. For those with ADHD who could overlook minor social signs, practicing identifying facial expressions, body language, and tone of voice might boost their capacity to interpret others' emotions.

Developing emotional vocabulary is vital for both self-awareness and empathy. By extending their ability to detect and describe emotions in themselves and others, individuals with ADHD can better understand and communicate about emotional experiences.

Practicing self-compassion is a vital component of growing both self-awareness and empathy. By treating oneself with love and understanding, individuals can build a more compassionate attitude towards others as well.

Lastly, engaging in group therapy or support groups can provide a supportive setting for increasing both self-awareness and empathy. Sharing experiences with others who encounter similar issues can develop self-reflection and mutual understanding.

By focusing on developing both self-awareness and empathy, individuals with ADHD can greatly enhance their emotional intelligence and resilience. These skills not only lead to greater emotional control but also boost interpersonal connections and general well-being.

Stress Management and Self-Compassion Practices

Stress management and self-compassion practices are crucial components of growing emotional resilience, particularly for those with ADHD who often experience heightened stress levels and may struggle with self-criticism. Developing effective techniques to manage stress and foster self-compassion can dramatically improve general well-being and emotional regulation.

Stress treatment for individuals with ADHD frequently begins with identifying personal stress causes. Common stressors could include time pressure, onerous tasks, social circumstances, or sensory overload. By recognizing these triggers, individuals can build proactive methods to lessen their influence. This can mean dividing huge work into smaller, manageable parts, employing time management tools, or establishing a sensory-friendly setting.

Implementing routines and structure can be a powerful stress management aid for persons with ADHD. Consistent daily routines help lessen decision fatigue and create a feeling of predictability, which can be comforting for persons who often feel overwhelmed by the demands of everyday living. This could involve establishing regular sleep schedules, lunch times, and allocated work or study periods.

Physical activity is another key stress management approach. Regular physical activity has been shown to lower stress, boost mood, and enhance cognitive performance - all of which can be particularly useful for those with ADHD. Engaging in activities that combine physical movement with mindfulness, such as yoga or tai chi, can be very useful in controlling stress and boosting focus.

Relaxation techniques are crucial tools in any stress management toolkit. Deep breathing exercises, progressive muscle relaxation, and guided visualization can assist individuals with ADHD calm their minds and bodies in situations of stress. These approaches can be particularly effective when done routinely, not just in response to stressful events.

Time management skills are vital for stress reduction in individuals with ADHD. Techniques such as the Pomodoro method (working in focused bursts with brief breaks), using visual schedules, or employing digital tools for task management might assist in alleviating the stress associated with time pressure and task completion.

Developing appropriate coping techniques is another crucial part of stress management. This could be engaging in creative activities, spending time in nature, practicing a hobby, or interacting with supportive friends and family. It's crucial for persons with ADHD to discover coping methods that work for them and to avoid maladaptive coping mechanisms like substance use or excessive screen time.

Mindfulness activities can be particularly beneficial for stress management in ADHD. Mindfulness helps individuals stay grounded in the present moment, lowering anxiety about the future or ruminating about the past. For persons with ADHD, shorter, more frequent mindfulness exercises or guided meditations could be more accessible than longer, unstructured activities.

Cognitive restructuring strategies can assist manage stress by shifting negative cognitive habits. This entails detecting and confronting stress-inducing thoughts and replacing them with more balanced, realistic perspectives. For persons with ADHD who can be inclined towards catastrophizing or negative self-talk, this can be a great strategy for stress reduction.

Turning to self-compassion practices, it's crucial to note that individuals with ADHD typically suffer from self-criticism and negative self-perception due to the obstacles associated with their disease. Developing self-compassion means treating oneself with the same care and understanding that one would offer to a good friend.

One fundamental self-compassion technique is attentive self-awareness. This entails monitoring one's thoughts and feelings without judgment. For those with ADHD, this might mean acknowledging disappointments or setbacks without harsh self-criticism, knowing that these feelings are part of the human condition.

Practicing positive self-talk is another crucial part of self-compassion. This entails intentionally replacing self-critical ideas with more supportive, encouraging internal dialogue. For example, instead of berating oneself for forgetting an assignment, an individual can say, "It's okay to make mistakes. I'm doing my best to improve my organization skills."

Developing a growth mentality is intimately tied to self-compassion. This involves viewing obstacles and disappointments as chances for learning and progress rather than as personal failures. For those with ADHD, adopting a growth mindset can help reframe challenges with focus or organization as areas for improvement rather than fundamental defects.

Self-care behaviors are an integral component of self-compassion. This involves prioritizing behaviors that enhance physical and emotional well-being, such as obtaining appropriate sleep, eating nutritious foods, engaging in fun hobbies, and setting boundaries in relationships and responsibilities.

Cultivating thankfulness can also increase self-compassion. By consistently highlighting good parts of oneself and one's life, individuals with ADHD can offset the inclination towards negative self-focus. This can mean keeping a gratitude book or simply taking a moment each day to dwell on things one likes about oneself.

Seeking assistance from others is a crucial element of both stress management and self-compassion. This can mean connecting with a therapist, joining a support group for those with ADHD, or establishing relationships with understanding friends and family members. Having a support network can provide affirmation, encouragement, and practical assistance in managing stress and practicing self-compassion.

By integrating these stress management and self-compassion strategies into daily life, individuals with ADHD can create stronger emotional resilience. These tactics not only help in managing the unique issues connected with ADHD but also contribute to general emotional well-being and life happiness.

Chapter Five

Navigating Relationships with ADHD

Communication Strategies for Emotional Situations

Adults with ADHD may encounter special obstacles when communicating in emotionally heated settings. Their predisposition towards impulsivity, trouble controlling emotions, and struggles with concentration can make effective communication seem like an overwhelming endeavor. However, with the correct tools and persistent practice, persons with ADHD can greatly improve their communication abilities, especially during sensitive situations.

One significant strategy is the use of the "pause and reflect" technique. This includes actively taking a moment to breathe and analyze one's thoughts and feelings before replying. For those with ADHD, this pause can be vital in preventing impulsive reactions that may worsen disputes or lead to misunderstandings. It enables time for the prefrontal brain to participate, facilitating more considered and measured reactions.

Active listening is another key ability for good communication. Adults with ADHD may have trouble with retaining concentration during talks, particularly when emotions are running high. Practicing active listening skills, such as keeping eye contact, nodding to show engagement, and repeating significant ideas back to the speaker, can assist in enhancing understanding and conveying empathy. This not only aids in understanding the other person's perspective but also helps in crafting more acceptable responses.

The usage of "I" phrases is particularly effective for those with ADHD in emotional situations. Instead of making accusatory statements that may generate defensiveness, expressing one's sentiments and needs might lead to more fruitful interactions. For example, saying "I feel overwhelmed when there are too many tasks to manage" is more effective than "You always give me too much work."

Developing emotional vocabulary is also vital. Many adults with ADHD fail to appropriately identify and express their emotions, which can lead to misunderstandings and frustration. By broadening their emotional vocabulary and practicing the identification of distinct emotional states, individuals may articulate their feelings more precisely, leading to better understanding and resolution of problems.

Time management in discussions is another crucial factor. Adults with ADHD may tend to ramble or go off on tangents, which can be particularly problematic in emotional situations. Setting time limitations for discussions, employing timers if required, and deciding on specific subjects to address can help keep conversations focused and effective.

Lastly, the use of visual aids or written communication can be helpful in emotional situations. For some adults with ADHD, absorbing verbal information in the heat of the moment might be problematic. Using diagrams, lists, or even exchanging written notes can provide a clearer, less emotionally charged mode of communication, allowing both sides to express themselves more effectively.

By following these tactics and consistently focusing on strengthening communication skills, adults with ADHD can navigate emotional situations more successfully, leading to healthier and more meaningful relationships in all areas of life.

Managing ADHD in Romantic Relationships

Romantic relationships may be both gratifying and stressful for persons with ADHD. The symptoms of ADHD, such as inattention, impulsivity, and emotional dysregulation, can dramatically disrupt the dynamics of romantic engagement. However, with knowledge, effort, and the correct tactics, individuals with ADHD can create and sustain healthy, meaningful love relationships.

One of the key obstacles in romantic relationships for persons with ADHD is maintaining consistency and reliability. Forgetfulness and time management concerns can lead to missed dates, forgotten anniversaries, or neglected tasks, which may strain the relationship. Implementing tools such as shared digital calendars, reminders, and alarms can help reduce these challenges. It's also vital for the individual with ADHD to communicate freely about their issues and work with their relationship to discover solutions that work for both parties.

Impulsivity in decision-making and communication can also cause issues in love relationships. Adults with ADHD could blurt out unpleasant statements without thinking or make rash financial decisions that harm the partnership. Developing ways to moderate impulsivity, such as the "pause and reflect" technique outlined above, might be effective. Additionally, creating agreed-upon rules for important decisions, such as discussing purchases over a particular amount, can help prevent impulsive behaviors that might negatively affect the relationship.

Emotional dysregulation is another feature of ADHD that can greatly influence romantic relationships. Mood swings heightened emotional responses, and trouble managing impatience can lead to confrontations and misunderstandings. Both partners must understand that these emotional reactions are often a symptom of ADHD rather than a reflection of the relationship itself. Developing emotional regulation tools, such as mindfulness practices or cognitive-behavioral tactics, can assist regulate these emotional fluctuations.

Hyperfocus, a frequent quality in those with ADHD, maybe both a blessing and a disaster in love relationships. While it can lead to strong periods of attention and affection towards a partner, it can also result in neglect when the individual becomes involved in other hobbies. Finding a balance and learning to shift focus purposefully is key. Setting aside designated "couple time" and employing reminders to switch focus can help maintain a healthy balance.

Sexual relationships can also be influenced by ADHD. Some adults with ADHD may experience hypersexuality, while others could struggle with keeping interest or focus during intimate moments.

Open communication about sexual wants and preferences is crucial, as is engaging with a therapist or counselor if necessary to address any sexual concerns associated with ADHD.

For the non-ADHD partner, understanding and patience are crucial. Educating themselves about ADHD and its influence on relationships can develop empathy and lessen irritation. It's also crucial for the non-ADHD partner to convey their demands clearly and set boundaries when required.

Couples therapy can be particularly effective for love relationships where one or both parties have ADHD. A therapist can help the couple create effective communication methods, work through ADHD-related issues, and build a better, more understanding partnership.

Ultimately, successful romantic relationships for individuals with ADHD involve self-awareness, open communication, mutual understanding, and a willingness to work together to discover techniques that meet both partners' needs. With effort and commitment, ADHD can be controlled effectively within the context of a loving, supportive love relationship.

Family Dynamics and Parenting with ADHD

ADHD can profoundly disrupt family dynamics, particularly when one or both parents have the illness. The challenges of ADHD symptoms can affect numerous parts of family life, from daily routines to long-term planning and emotional connections. However, with adequate education, methods, and support, families can succeed despite the problems provided by ADHD.

For parents with ADHD, organizing and managing home tasks can be extremely tough. Symptoms such as forgetfulness, trouble with time management, and struggles with maintaining order can contribute to a chaotic home environment. Implementing structured procedures for household management is vital. This might include using visual timetables, setting up reminder systems, and dividing work into smaller, achievable chunks. Involving all family members in designing and maintaining these systems helps foster a sense of collaboration and shared responsibility.

Consistency in parenting can be another big problem for adults with ADHD. The impulsivity and emotional dysregulation associated with ADHD might lead to inconsistent discipline or difficulty in following through with consequences. Developing a clear, agreed-upon set of family rules and punishments, and employing visual reminders of these norms, can help preserve consistency. It's also crucial for parents with ADHD to focus on their emotional regulation abilities to offer a stable emotional environment for their children.

Time management in family life is vital, and this can be particularly tough for parents with ADHD. Tardiness to school functions, missed appointments, or rushed mornings can create stress for the entire family. Utilizing tools such as family calendars, setting numerous alarms, and preparing for the next day the night before can assist manage time more successfully. It's also beneficial to build buffer time for transitions and unexpected delays.

For children in families where one or both parents have ADHD, recognizing their parent's illness is vital. Age-appropriate teaching about ADHD can help youngsters develop empathy and patience. It's also vital for parents to demonstrate self-compassion and transparency about their struggles, telling their children that it's alright to suffer and ask for help.

When both a parent and a child have ADHD, it can generate unique dynamics. On one side, the parent may have a stronger awareness of the child's challenges. On the contrary, it may lead to heightened irritation when both are battling with comparable issues. In these situations, it's crucial to focus on strengths, celebrate minor triumphs, and work together to identify ways that work for the family as a whole.

Balancing attention among siblings can be tough, especially if one child has ADHD and others do not. Parents should attempt to spend one-on-one time with each child regularly and encourage open communication about emotions of fairness and attention distribution.

Self-care for parents with ADHD is vital but often forgotten. The pressures of parenthood can exacerbate ADHD symptoms, leading to exhaustion. Prioritizing self-care activities, getting assistance from partners or extended family, and maybe enrolling in individual treatment can help parents maintain their well-being, which in turn benefits the entire family.

Family therapy can be effective in treating ADHD-related difficulties within the family system. A therapist can help family members improve communication, build problem-solving skills, and devise methods tailored to the family's unique requirements.

Lastly, families impacted by ADHD must connect with support networks. This can include support groups for parents with ADHD, internet communities, or local organizations that give resources and education about ADHD. These ties can provide vital emotional support, practical counsel, and a feeling of community.

While ADHD can provide substantial obstacles in family life, it can also bring distinct assets such as creativity, excitement, and a propensity to think outside the box. By concentrating on these characteristics, applying effective techniques, and promoting open communication and mutual support, families can not only deal with ADHD but thrive, establishing a caring, understanding, and dynamic family atmosphere.

Chapter Six

Emotional Regulation in the Workplace

Managing Emotional Challenges in Professional Settings

For those with ADHD, handling emotional issues in work situations can be extremely complex. The job often provides unique stressors and responsibilities that might exacerbate ADHD symptoms and emotional dysregulation. However, with the correct tactics and understanding, it's possible to negotiate these hurdles efficiently and succeed in professional contexts.

One of the biggest emotional obstacles in the job for those with ADHD is managing frustration and impatience. The need to focus on tasks that may not be intrinsically entertaining, coupled with the pressure to fulfill deadlines, can lead to heightened feelings of irritation. To overcome this, it's necessary to adopt tactics for task management that correspond with ADHD characteristics. This can mean breaking larger projects into smaller, more manageable chunks, utilizing visual aids like flowcharts or mind maps to organize information, or applying the Pomodoro Technique to work in focused bursts with regular breaks.

Impulsivity, another prevalent trait in ADHD, can lead to emotional outbursts or inappropriate comments in professional contexts. To manage this, individuals can practice the "pause and reflect" strategy. This entails taking a minute to contemplate the potential ramifications of an action or speech before proceeding. Developing a personal mantra or employing visual clues (such as a tiny object on the desk) might serve as reminders to halt and consider before reacting.

Anxiety is typically a significant emotional barrier for those with ADHD on the job. This can originate from anxieties about underperforming, missing deadlines or making mistakes. To manage work-related anxiety, it's useful to adopt a disciplined approach to tasks and time management. This can include using digital tools for reminders and organization, establishing thorough to-do lists, and setting realistic objectives and expectations. Regular check-ins with supervisors or mentors can also help ease anxiety by establishing alignment on priorities and expectations.

Emotional overwhelm is another typical difficulty, particularly in fast-paced or high-pressure professional contexts. To remedy this, individuals with ADHD can benefit from creating a "sensory-friendly" workspace. This can mean using noise-canceling headphones, altering lighting, or locating a quieter workplace when available.

Additionally, adopting mindfulness practices, such as deep breathing exercises or brief meditation sessions, might help manage feelings of overwhelm in the workplace.

Rejection sensitivity, a feature typically associated with ADHD, can lead to heightened emotional reactions to perceived criticism or negative feedback on the job. To manage this, it's crucial to develop ways for reframing comments as chances for progress rather than personal attacks. This can mean asking for precise, practical comments and concentrating on tangible strategies for change. Additionally, developing a support network within the job might provide a barrier against emotions of rejection or inadequacy.

Time blindness, or difficulty recognizing and managing time, can lead to stress and emotional distress in professional contexts. To solve this, individuals with ADHD can benefit from external time management tools such as visual timers, calendar apps with notifications, or even analog clocks placed strategically in the workspace. Breaking the workday into clearly defined blocks of time for certain tasks can also assist manage time-related stress.

Emotional management in meetings and collaborative settings can be particularly tough for those with ADHD. Strategies for success in these settings could include preparing notes or questions in advance, using fidget tools discreetly to manage restlessness, and using active listening skills to keep interested. It can also be good to communicate with colleagues about preferred communication patterns, such as the requirement for clear, succinct instructions or written follow-ups after verbal discussions.

Managing the emotional effect of losses or mistakes is vital for working success. Individuals with ADHD may be prone to extreme sentiments of disappointment or self-criticism when things don't go as planned. Developing a growth attitude and practicing self-compassion is vital in these situations. This might involve reframing failures as learning opportunities, acknowledging progress and efforts rather than merely outcomes, and building a personal "recovery plan" for bouncing back from setbacks.

Lastly, it's crucial to acknowledge the function of self-care in addressing emotional issues in the workplace. This includes maintaining a healthy work-life balance, engaging in regular physical activity, obtaining appropriate sleep, and pursuing hobbies or interests outside of work. These techniques can promote emotional resilience and a buffer against work-related stress.

By following these tactics and continuously refining them based on personal experiences, individuals with ADHD can effectively manage emotional problems in professional contexts. This not only leads to enhanced job performance but also helps to overall well-being and career happiness.

Disclosure and Accommodation Strategies

The decision to reveal ADHD in the workplace and seek accommodations is a very personal one that demands careful consideration. While disclosure can lead to better understanding and assistance, it also comes with potential consequences. Understanding the advantages and cons of disclosure and learning how to appropriately request accommodations are key skills for individuals with ADHD in professional situations.

When considering disclosure, it's vital to analyze the potential benefits. These may include:

1. Access to formal accommodations under disability laws

2. Increased understanding from superiors and colleagues

3. The ability to openly discuss issues and solutions

4. Reduced stress from masking the condition

5. Potential for personalized performance evaluations

However, there are also potential downsides to consider:

1. Risk of stigma or prejudice

2. Misconceptions about ADHD and its impact on work performance

3. Concerns regarding job security or advancement opportunities

4. Oversharing of personal information in a business situation

Before deciding to reveal, it's vital to examine the company's policies on disability and accommodations. Understanding your legal rights under the Americans with Disabilities Act (ADA) or comparable laws in your nation is also vital. These regulations often oblige employers to make reasonable accommodations for employees with impairments, including ADHD.

If you decide to reveal, time is essential. Some choose to reveal during the job process to ensure they may receive appropriate accommodations from the start. Others wait until they've established themselves in the role. There's no one-size-fits-all method, and the decision should be based on individual circumstances and comfort level.

When disclosing, it's vital to focus on how ADHD affects your work specifically, rather than providing a general explanation of the disease. Prepare a clear, straightforward description of your issues and the accommodations that could help you perform at your best. For example:

"I have ADHD, which sometimes makes it challenging for me to filter out distractions in open office environments. I've found that using noise-canceling headphones significantly improves my focus and productivity. Would it be possible for me to use these during work hours?"

When asking for accommodations, be explicit about what you require and how it will help your work performance. Some frequent accommodations for ADHD in the workplace include:

1. Flexible work hours or the option to work remotely

2. A quiet workstation or authorization to wear noise-canceling headphones

3. Written instructions or follow-ups after verbal meetings

4. Use of organizational tools or apps

5. Regular check-ins with supervisors for feedback and priority-setting

6. Extended deadlines or dividing major tasks into smaller phases

7. Permission to use fidget gadgets or standing desks

It's vital to approach accommodation requests in terms of how they will benefit both you and the firm. For example:

"Having a second computer monitor would allow me to keep my task list visible at all times, reducing the likelihood of missed deadlines and improving my overall productivity."

When discussing accommodations with your employer, be open to discovering creative solutions that work for both parties. Sometimes, the most successful accommodations are ones that are suited to your individual function and company culture.

If you're uncomfortable disclosing straight to your supervisor, consider discussing it with the Human Resources department first. They can often provide advice on the disclosure procedure and help expedite accommodation requests.

After disclosure and implementation of accommodations, it's necessary to follow up and analyze their efficacy. Be prepared to adapt your strategies as needed and continue communication with your employer about what's working and what might need to be modified.

Remember that disclosure is not a one-time event but a continuing process. As your function or the nature of your work changes, you may need to revisit the conversation concerning accommodations.

Lastly, it's vital to maintain professionalism throughout the disclosure and accommodation process. Focus on your abilities and how adjustments might help you achieve your best, rather than obsessing over limitations. By handling the situation proactively and constructively, you can create a more supportive and productive work environment for yourself and potentially pave the way for increased knowledge of ADHD in your company.

Building a Supportive Work Environment

Creating a supportive work environment is vital for those with ADHD to thrive professionally. While personal methods and modifications are crucial, the entire workplace culture and environment have a vital impact on treating ADHD symptoms and supporting emotional well-being. Building a supportive work environment includes efforts from both the individual with ADHD and their coworkers and managers.

For those with ADHD, taking an active role in setting their work environment is crucial. This starts with self-advocacy and straightforward communication about needs and preferences. It's crucial to articulate specific difficulties and suggest solutions. For example, if background noise is a big distractor, advocating the implementation of a quiet zone or the usage of white noise machines in the office can be advantageous.

Educating colleagues and supervisors about ADHD can be an effective strategy to generate understanding and support. This doesn't necessarily mean reporting your diagnosis if you're not comfortable doing so. Instead, you might provide basic information about ADHD in the workplace, possibly by suggesting relevant articles or webinars to the HR department or during team meetings. This can help build a more informed and empathetic work atmosphere.

Building great relationships with colleagues is another key part of having a supportive environment. This requires being a good team player, offering help when feasible, and showing appreciation for others' support. When coworkers understand your work style and see your devotion to the team, they're more likely to be supportive when you experience ADHD-related issues.

For managers and organizations, building a supportive workplace for employees with ADHD (and neurodiversity in general) entails many critical strategies:

1. Flexible Work Arrangements: Offering options for flexible hours or remote work can be extremely advantageous for those with ADHD who may have varied peak productivity times or desire a calmer work environment.

2. Clear Communication: Providing clear, written instructions and expectations can assist employees with ADHD to stay on track and reduce concern over misunderstandings.

3. Structured Feedback: Regular, constructive feedback sessions can assist employees with ADHD in understanding their performance and areas for development, decreasing ambiguity and stress.

4. Diverse Work Spaces: Creating a variety of work settings within the office, such as quiet zones, collaborative spaces, and areas for movement or standing workstations, can suit varied work styles and needs.

5. Emphasis on Outcomes: Focusing on work outcomes rather than inflexible processes can allow employees with ADHD to choose work techniques that suit their specific strengths and problems.

6. Professional Development: Offering training in time management, organization, and other pertinent skills can benefit all employees, even those with ADHD.

7. Mental Health Support: Providing access to mental health resources and establishing a culture that values mental well-being can be particularly beneficial for employees with ADHD who may battle with anxiety or sadness.

8. Neurodiversity Training: Implementing organization-wide training on neurodiversity helps build a more inclusive and understanding working culture.

Creating a friendly work environment also requires addressing and eliminating stigma. This can be achieved by open discussions about mental health and neurodiversity, challenging preconceptions, and highlighting the particular assets that persons with ADHD can offer to the workplace, such as creativity, problem-solving skills, and the ability to hyperfocus on stimulating tasks.

Technology may play a big part in developing a supportive workplace. Implementing project management tools that provide visual representations of work and deadlines can be helpful for employees with ADHD. Similarly, employing collaboration systems that allow for diverse communication modalities (e.g., chat, video, email) can accommodate individual preferences and strengths.

It's also vital to identify and celebrate varied thinking patterns. Individuals with ADHD can provide unique insights and inventive solutions to challenges. Encouraging and recognizing these efforts can not only benefit the individual but also encourage innovation inside the organization.

Creating mentorship or buddy systems might be extremely effective. Pairing individuals with ADHD with more experienced colleagues who can offer guidance and support can help navigate professional problems and promote a sense of belonging.

Lastly, building a culture of constant development and receptivity to feedback is vital. Regularly requesting comments from employees on the working environment and policies can assist in identifying areas for improvement and ensuring that the needs of diverse employees, including those with ADHD, are being fulfilled.

By implementing these measures and developing a culture of understanding and support, organizations can create an atmosphere where individuals with ADHD can succeed professionally. This not only benefits the individuals themselves but also leads to a more varied, inclusive, and inventive workplace for all employees.

Chapter Seven

Lifestyle Optimization for Emotional Balance

Sleep Hygiene for Mood Stability

Sleep hygiene plays a critical role in maintaining emotional balance, particularly for those with ADHD who typically struggle with sleep-related disorders. Poor sleep can exacerbate ADHD symptoms, leading to greater emotional dysregulation, impatience, and difficulties concentrating. Conversely, proper sleep hygiene can considerably increase mood stability and overall functioning.

One of the most important parts of sleep hygiene is having a consistent sleep pattern. This implies going to bed and waking up at the same time every day, even on weekends. For persons with ADHD, who may struggle with time management and routine, this can be problematic but is crucial for regulating the body's internal clock or circadian rhythm. Setting alarms for both bedtime and wake-up time can be beneficial in creating this pattern.

Creating a soothing nighttime ritual is another crucial component of healthy sleep hygiene. This practice should begin approximately an hour before the targeted sleep time and include calming activities such as reading, moderate stretching, or listening to peaceful music. For those with ADHD, it's particularly crucial to avoid stimulating activities like vigorous exercise, work-related tasks, or engaging with electronic devices during this wind-down period.

Speaking of electronic gadgets, the blue light emitted by smartphones, tablets, and computers might interfere with the generation of melatonin, the hormone that regulates sleep. Individuals with ADHD, who may be more sensitive to sensory input, should be especially cautious of this. Implementing a "no screens" rule at least an hour before bedtime can be advantageous. If device use is necessary, utilizing blue light filtering applications or glasses can help lessen the damage.

The sleep environment itself is vital for proper sleep hygiene. The bedroom should be cold, dark, and quiet. For persons with ADHD who may be easily distracted by ambient stimuli, adopting blackout curtains, white noise generators, or earplugs can provide a more favorable sleep environment. It's also vital to reserve the bed for sleep and intimacy only, avoiding activities like working or watching TV in bed, which might alter the brain's association of the bed with sleep.

Caffeine and other stimulants can dramatically impair sleep quality, especially for those with

ADHD who may already battle with hyperactivity. It's suggested to avoid coffee in the afternoon and evening. Similarly, while alcohol may seem to help in falling asleep, it generally leads to disordered sleep later in the night. Establishing a cut-off time for both coffee and alcohol usage can improve sleep quality.

Regular exercise can considerably enhance sleep quality, but timing is key. For persons with ADHD, who may benefit from the focus-enhancing effects of exercise, it's better to participate in physical activity early in the day. Intense activity too close to bedtime might be stimulating and make it harder to fall asleep.

Stress and anxiety often contribute to sleep issues, and this can be particularly obvious for persons with ADHD who may battle with racing thoughts or concerns. Incorporating stress-reduction practices into the daily routine, such as mindfulness meditation, deep breathing exercises, or journaling, can help calm the mind before bed.

For some individuals with ADHD, racing thoughts at bedtime can be a substantial barrier to sleep. Keeping a notepad by the bed to jot down any ideas or anxieties will help cleanse the mind. This "brain dump" technique can be particularly beneficial in lowering nocturnal tension and fostering relaxation.

It's also crucial to be attentive to sleep position and comfort. Investing in a supportive mattress and pillows can make a substantial impact on sleep quality. Some individuals with ADHD find that weighted blankets create a sense of comfort and can aid with falling asleep quickly.

If sleep troubles persist despite proper sleep hygiene techniques, it may be worth discussing with a healthcare physician. Some individuals with ADHD may benefit from sleep aids or adjustments to their ADHD medication regimen to enhance sleep quality.

Lastly, it's vital to pursue sleep hygiene with patience and persistence. It may take time for the body to acclimate to new sleep habits, and there may be setbacks along the road. For persons with ADHD, who may struggle with consistency, scheduling reminders or using sleep tracking apps can help maintain appropriate sleep hygiene practices over time.

By prioritizing sleep hygiene, persons with ADHD can greatly improve their mood stability, emotional regulation, and general quality of life. Good sleep provides a foundation for better control of ADHD symptoms and enhanced emotional equilibrium throughout the day.

Nutrition and Exercise as Emotional Regulation Tools

Nutrition and exercise have crucial roles in emotional regulation, particularly for persons with ADHD. The food we consume and the physical activities we engage in can significantly alter our brain chemistry, energy levels, and general emotional stability. By optimizing nutrition and combining regular exercise, persons with ADHD can develop a stable basis for greater emotional regulation.

Starting with diet, it's crucial to recognize that the brain requires a consistent flow of nutrients to function efficiently. For those with ADHD, who may already battle with neurotransmitter abnormalities, a well-balanced diet is vital. Complex carbs, found in whole grains, fruits, and vegetables, give a continuous release of glucose to the brain, helping to maintain consistent energy levels and mood throughout the day. This is particularly crucial for persons with ADHD who may be prone to energy dumps and mood changes.

Protein is another vital component of a brain-healthy diet. Proteins contain amino acids, which are precursors to neurotransmitters like dopamine and norepinephrine - both of which play crucial roles in attention and mood regulation. Including lean proteins such as fish, poultry, lentils, and nuts in each meal will help regulate mood and increase focus.

Omega-3 fatty acids, notably EPA and DHA found in fatty fish, flaxseeds, and walnuts, have been demonstrated to have a good impact on brain function and may help ease ADHD symptoms. Some research suggests that omega-3 supplementation helps improve emotional regulation and reduce impulsivity in individuals with ADHD.

It's equally vital to be careful of meals that may increase ADHD symptoms and emotional instability. Processed foods heavy in sugar and chemical additives can lead to rapid increases and drops in blood sugar, which can promote mood swings and irritation. Similarly, while coffee may provide a momentary boost in focus, it can also cause anxiety and alter sleep patterns if ingested in excess or too late in the day.

Maintaining steady blood sugar levels is vital for mood management. This can be achieved by eating frequent, balanced meals and healthy snacks throughout the day. For persons with ADHD who may struggle with meal planning or tend to skip meals, providing reminders or preparing meals in advance might be helpful methods.

Hydration also has a crucial influence on mood regulation. Even slight dehydration can influence cognitive function and mood. Individuals with ADHD should attempt to drink lots of water throughout the day, potentially setting reminders or utilizing marked water bottles to guarantee optimal consumption.

Moving on to exercise, regular physical activity is one of the most effective natural treatments for ADHD and emotional management. Exercise boosts the production of neurotransmitters like dopamine and norepinephrine, which are commonly lacking in patients with ADHD. This spike in brain chemistry can contribute to enhanced mood, better focus, and fewer symptoms of anxiety and sadness.

Aerobic workouts, such as jogging, cycling, or swimming, are particularly good for those with ADHD. These activities boost heart rate and blood supply to the brain, potentially increasing executive function and emotional regulation. Even short bursts of intensive activity, like high-intensity interval training (HIIT), can have significant mood-boosting effects.

Strength training can also be good for emotional management. The focus necessary for good form and the sense of success from progressive gains can promote self-esteem and give a healthy outlet for excess energy or frustration.

Mind-body therapies like yoga or tai chi integrate physical activity with awareness, delivering multiple advantages for those with ADHD. These routines can improve bodily awareness, reduce tension, and strengthen emotional management skills.

For people who struggle with consistency, finding enjoyable types of exercise is crucial. This might encompass team sports, dance lessons, martial arts, or outdoor hobbies like hiking or rock climbing. The social aspect of group exercise might bring additional emotional advantages and motivation.

Incorporating movement throughout the day, rather than relying primarily on planned exercise sessions, might be particularly useful for those with ADHD. This can include taking short walking breaks, using a standing desk, or conducting fast stretching routines between activities.

It's crucial to emphasize that while nutrition and exercise are significant tools for emotional regulation, they function best as part of a holistic therapy approach. For persons with ADHD, these lifestyle factors should complement, not replace, existing therapies such as medication and therapy.

Lastly, it's vital to approach nutrition and exercise with a mindset of self-compassion and flexibility. Perfection is not the objective, and little, persistent modifications can lead to major improvements over time. By prioritizing healthful eating habits and frequent physical activity, persons with ADHD can develop a strong foundation for enhanced emotional regulation and general well-being.

Creating an ADHD-Friendly Environment at Home and Work

Creating an ADHD-friendly environment at home and work is crucial for managing symptoms and promoting emotional balance. The physical space we inhabit can significantly impact our ability to focus, regulate emotions, and maintain productivity. By optimizing our surroundings, individuals with ADHD can reduce distractions, minimize stress, and create a supportive atmosphere for better emotional regulation.

Starting with the home environment, organization is key. Clutter can be particularly overwhelming for individuals with ADHD, leading to increased stress and difficulty focusing. Implementing a system of organization that is both functional and easy to maintain is essential. This might involve:

1. Designated spaces for important items like keys, wallets, and phones to reduce the stress of misplacing things.

2. Clear, labeled storage solutions for different categories of items.

3. Regular decluttering sessions to prevent accumulation of unnecessary items.

4. Use of visual cues, such as color-coding or picture labels, to make organization intuitive.

The layout of living spaces can also impact emotional regulation. Creating distinct areas for different activities can help with task initiation and completion. For example, having a dedicated workspace separate from relaxation areas can help maintain work-life balance and reduce the stress of constantly shifting between modes.

Lighting plays a crucial role in mood and focus. Natural light is ideal, but where that's not possible, full-spectrum light bulbs can mimic natural light and help regulate circadian rhythms. Individuals with ADHD may be sensitive to harsh or flickering lights, so choosing warm, steady lighting options can create a more soothing environment.

Noise management is another important aspect of an ADHD-friendly home. While some individuals with ADHD work well with background noise, others find it distracting. Implementing sound-absorbing materials like rugs or curtains, using white noise machines, or designating quiet zones in the home can help create a more focused environment.

Temperature and air quality also impact comfort and concentration. Maintaining a cool, well-ventilated space can prevent the discomfort and restlessness that can exacerbate ADHD symptoms.

In the workplace, many of the same principles apply, but there may be additional considerations:

1. Workspace organization: A clean, organized desk with only essential items visible can reduce visual distractions. Using drawer organizers, file systems, and digital organization tools can help maintain order.

2. Ergonomics: Comfortable, supportive seating and proper desk height are crucial for maintaining focus and reducing physical discomfort that can lead to emotional frustration.

3. Sensory considerations: If possible, choosing a workspace away from high-traffic areas or using noise-canceling headphones can help manage auditory distractions. Some individuals with ADHD benefit from standing desks or balance ball chairs, which allow for movement while working.

4. Time management tools: Visual timers, analog clocks, or time-tracking apps prominently displayed can help with time blindness, a common challenge for those with ADHD.

5. Task management systems: Whether digital or physical, having a clear system for tracking tasks and deadlines is crucial. This might involve using project management software, a bulletin board with task cards, or a combination of methods.

6. Break spaces: Designating areas for short breaks can help with emotional regulation throughout the workday. This might be a quiet corner for meditation or a space for brief physical activity.

Technology can be both a help and a hindrance for individuals with ADHD. While it can provide valuable tools for organization and productivity, it can also be a source of distraction. Setting up technology in an ADHD-friendly way might involve:

1. Using website blockers or app timers to limit access to distracting content during work hours.
2. Customizing notification settings to minimize non-essential interruptions.

3. Utilizing productivity apps that align with ADHD-friendly work strategies, such as the Pomodoro technique.

Creating an emotionally supportive environment also involves considering the people around us. At home, this might mean having open conversations with family members about ADHD needs and working together to create a supportive atmosphere. In the workplace, it could involve discussing accommodations with supervisors or HR, such as flexible work hours or the ability to use noise-canceling headphones.

It's important to remember that an ADHD-friendly environment is not static. As needs change or new challenges arise, the environment may need to be adjusted. Regular reassessment of what's working and what isn't can help maintain an optimal space for emotional regulation and productivity.

Lastly, incorporating elements of nature into both home and work environments can have a calming effect. This might involve houseplants, nature-themed artwork, or even a small desktop water feature. These elements can provide a sense of calm and serve as natural attention reset points throughout the day.

By thoughtfully creating ADHD-friendly environments at home and work, individuals can significantly reduce daily stressors, improve focus, and create a foundation for better emotional regulation. While it may take time and experimentation to find the optimal setup, the benefits in terms of reduced anxiety, improved productivity, and overall emotional well-being are well worth the effort.

Chapter Eight

Technology and Tools for Emotional Management

Apps and Digital Tools for Mood Tracking and Regulation

In the digital era, a profusion of apps and digital tools have evolved to assist individuals, particularly those with ADHD, in tracking and regulating their emotions. These technological aids can provide valuable insights into emotional patterns, enable real-time interventions, and help overall emotional management tactics.

Mood-tracking applications are at the vanguard of this digital revolution in emotional management. These apps allow users to register their emotional states routinely, typically many times a day. Many of these apps employ a combination of text entries, number scales, and even emoji-based systems to make mood logging easy and intuitive. For those with ADHD, who may struggle with constant self-monitoring, these applications can act as helpful reminders and give an easy way to record mood swings.

Advanced mood-tracking apps go beyond simple logging to enable analysis of mood patterns over time. They may generate graphs and reports that can help users and their healthcare practitioners discover triggers, patterns, and potential areas for intervention. Some apps even use machine learning algorithms to forecast probable mood shifts based on previous data and present inputs, allowing for proactive management tactics.

Mindfulness and meditation applications have also become popular tools for emotional management. These applications offer guided meditations, breathing exercises, and mindfulness practices adapted to varied requirements and time limits. For persons with ADHD, who may find traditional meditation problematic, several of these apps provide shorter sessions or movement-based mindfulness activities that might be more engaging and accessible.

Cognitive Behavioral Therapy (CBT) based applications give digital versions of CBT approaches, which can be particularly effective for regulating the negative thought patterns typically linked with ADHD. These apps could contain elements like thought journals, cognitive restructuring exercises, and behavioral activation tools. The digital format enables easy access to these strategies in periods of emotional distress.

Time management and productivity tools, while not explicitly developed for emotional regulation, can play a key role in lowering stress and overwhelm for those with ADHD. Apps that use strategies like the

Pomodoro method (work sprints followed by brief breaks) or that provide visual representations of tasks and deadlines can assist manage the time blindness and procrastination typically associated with ADHD, hence lowering anxiety and aggravation.

Social support applications connect users with peers who are grappling with similar issues. These platforms can provide a sense of community, offer peer support, and allow for the sharing of coping skills. For persons with ADHD, who may sometimes feel lonely in their challenges, these applications can be a great source of emotional support and practical advice.

Habit-tracking apps can be repurposed for emotional management by allowing users to track actions that affect mood, such as sleep, exercise, or medication adherence. By visualizing the connection between these habits and emotional states, individuals with ADHD can receive insights into what lifestyle choices most significantly affect their mood stability.

Some apps focus on specific emotional difficulties common with ADHD, such as anger management or anxiety reduction. These personalized aids generally mix educational content with interactive activities and coping strategies suited to the specific emotion.

Gamified apps for emotional regulation harness the compelling characteristics of games to teach and reinforce emotional management skills. These can be particularly useful for those with ADHD, who may respond strongly to the immediate feedback and incentive systems characteristic in game contexts.

Virtual coaching apps use AI to deliver personalized ideas and interventions depending on user input. While not a replacement for real therapists, these applications can give on-demand help and direction for managing day-to-day emotional issues.

It's crucial to emphasize that while these digital tools can be immensely beneficial, they should be utilized as part of a comprehensive emotional management approach, ideally under the advice of a healthcare professional. Privacy problems should also be considered while utilizing apps that collect sensitive personal data.

For individuals with ADHD, the key to successfully using these apps and digital tools is choosing ones that correspond with their requirements and interests. This can require experimenting with multiple apps to find the ideal combination of features, user experience, and engagement level. The goal is to find tools that not only provide significant insights and support but are also pleasant and easy to use frequently.

As technology continues to progress, we should expect to see even more complex and tailored digital tools for emotional regulation. These may include integration with other health data, more advanced prediction skills, and even augmented reality features to provide in-the-moment emotional support.

By leveraging these digital tools successfully, persons with ADHD can obtain deeper insight into their emotional patterns, access assistance, and interventions when needed, and build more effective techniques for long-term emotional regulation.

Wearable Technology for Emotional Awareness

Wearable technology has altered the way we monitor and manage numerous aspects of our health, and emotional awareness is no exception. For individuals with ADHD, who often struggle with emotional control and self-awareness, wearable gadgets offer a unique chance to gain real-time insights into their emotional moods and physiological responses.

One of the most common types of wearable technology utilized for emotional awareness is the wristwatch or fitness tracker. These devices often come equipped with heart rate monitors and may track variations in heart rate variability (HRV). HRV is a critical indicator of the body's stress response and can provide valuable information about emotional states. For those with ADHD, who may not always be consciously aware of their stress levels, these devices can function as early warning systems, alerting the wearer to heightened stress before it progresses into emotional dysregulation.

More modern wearables go beyond heart rate monitoring to track additional physiological signs of emotional states. These may include skin conductance (which detects small changes in sweating), body temperature, and even muscle tension. By merging several data sources, these gadgets can provide a more thorough picture of the wearer's emotional state. For individuals with ADHD, who may have trouble identifying and describing their feelings, these objective evaluations might serve as useful clues for emotional self-reflection.

Some wearable technologies are specifically developed for stress management and emotional regulation. These might incorporate features like guided breathing exercises that sync with the user's current heart rate, vibration alerts for mindfulness reminders, or even mild tactile input to assist ground the wearer during moments of emotional intensity. For those with ADHD, who may benefit from external cues for self-regulation, these features can provide early treatments to minimize emotional escalation.

Wearable EEG (electroencephalogram) gadgets are an emerging technology that allows direct insight into brain function. While not yet as widespread or user-friendly as other wearables, these devices have the potential to deliver precise information regarding attention, focus, and emotional states. For persons with ADHD, EEG wristbands could offer significant input on cognitive states throughout the day, potentially helping to pinpoint optimal periods for particular sorts of work or activities.

Sleep tracking is another essential aspect of many wearable devices that might indirectly support emotional awareness and management. Given the significant connection between sleep quality and emotional stability, particularly for persons with ADHD, tracking sleep patterns might provide insights into potential causes for emotional dysregulation. Some powerful sleep monitors may even discern between sleep stages, delivering a more detailed knowledge of sleep quality.

The data collected by wearable devices is commonly linked with smartphone apps, providing users with extensive statistics and trends over time. For those with ADHD, who may have difficulty with constant self-monitoring, this automatic data collecting and analysis can be very beneficial. It enables the detection of patterns and triggers that might not be visible through self-observation alone.

Some wearable gadgets contain social aspects, allowing users to interact with others for support and incentive. For persons with ADHD, who may benefit from external accountability, these social features can motivate frequent usage of the device and engagement with emotional awareness practices.

As wearable technology continues to evolve, we're seeing the emergence of more specialized devices for emotional awareness and regulation. For example, some wearables employ mild vibrations or sounds to guide the wearer through mindfulness exercises or grounding techniques. Others are designed to be worn on multiple regions of the body, such as the wrist or chest, to gather different sorts of physiological data.

It's vital to highlight that while wearable technology can provide helpful data, understanding this information in the context of ADHD and individual experiences is crucial. Working with a healthcare provider or therapist to evaluate the data and implement appropriate therapies based on the insights gleaned from wearables can be incredibly valuable.

Privacy and data security are critical considerations when employing wearable technology for emotional awareness. Users should be careful of the types of data being collected and how it's being stored and shared. For those with ADHD, who may be prone to impulsivity, it's particularly crucial to thoroughly consider privacy settings and data-sharing alternatives.

The future of wearable technology for emotional awareness is exciting. We may see devices that can forecast emotional states based on a mix of physiological data and contextual circumstances, or wearables that can automatically perform individualized interventions based on identified emotional states. For those with ADHD, these developments potentially give unprecedented help for emotional regulation in daily life.

In conclusion, wearable technology is a valuable tool for boosting emotional awareness and supporting regulation measures for those with ADHD. By providing objective data, real-time feedback, and timely treatments, these devices can supplement established therapy approaches and allow users to take a more active role in regulating their emotional well-being.

Virtual Reality and Biofeedback Applications

Virtual Reality (VR) and biofeedback applications are cutting-edge technologies in the realm of emotional management, enabling immersive and interactive experiences that can be particularly beneficial for those with ADHD. These technologies provide unique chances for training emotional regulation abilities in controlled, yet realistic contexts, while also delivering rapid feedback on physiological responses.

Virtual Reality for emotional management often incorporates immersive, computer-generated settings that imitate real-world scenarios or create wholly new experiences designed to elicit and help control emotional reactions. For persons with ADHD, who may struggle with emotional regulation in day-to-day situations, VR offers a safe area to practice coping methods without real-world consequences.

One of the key applications of VR in emotional management is exposure therapy. This entails gradually introducing individuals to circumstances that provoke emotional responses, allowing them to practice regulating strategies in a controlled context. For example, someone with ADHD who has anxiety in social circumstances might utilize a VR application that replicates various social events, from one-on-one interactions to larger group settings. By continuously practicing these events in VR, kids can gain more confidence and emotional control that translates to real-world circumstances.

VR can also be utilized to create peaceful surroundings for relaxation and stress reduction. These could include tranquil natural settings like beaches or forests, or abstract spaces developed particularly for mindfulness training. For persons with ADHD, who may find it tough to focus during traditional meditation or relaxation activities, the immersive quality of VR can assist sustain attention and eliminate distractions.

Some VR applications mix emotional management with cognitive training exercises. These could involve tasks that require focus and emotional management simultaneously, such as completing puzzles or negotiating obstacles while managing virtual pressures. This form of multitasking in a controlled environment can be particularly good for those with ADHD, helping them develop techniques for maintaining emotional balance while under cognitive pressure.

Biofeedback, typically linked with VR experiences, gives real-time information regarding physiological processes such as heart rate, skin conductance, or brain activity. This rapid input allows users to witness the direct impact of their emotional states and regulatory attempts on their bodies. For those with ADHD, who may have difficulties identifying small changes in their emotional or physiological states, biofeedback can serve as a valuable tool for developing more self-awareness.

In a VR biofeedback application, users would see visual representations of their physiological data overlaid on the virtual environment. For example, a user's heart rate might be represented by the pace of a flowing river or the intensity of a luminous ball. As students practice relaxation techniques, they can observe immediate changes in these visual representations, offering physical evidence of their ability to impact their emotional and physiological states.

Some VR and biofeedback programs employ gamification to make emotional control practice more enjoyable. This might feature narrative-driven experiences where emotional management is crucial to going through a story, or competitive components where maintaining emotional balance leads to higher scores. For those with ADHD, who frequently respond well to instant feedback and rewards, these gamified techniques can enhance motivation and engagement with emotional management strategies.

Virtual reality can also be utilized to imitate working events, helping individuals with ADHD to learn emotional regulation in professional contexts. This can include virtual presentations, uncomfortable talks with colleagues, or high-pressure job circumstances. By rehearsing these events in VR, users can build more confidence and emotional resilience for real-world professional obstacles.

Emerging research is examining the use of VR and biofeedback for ADHD assessment and therapy. Some programs try to give more ecologically valid assessments of attention and impulse control by replicating real-world contexts. Others focus on neurofeedback training, where users learn to adjust their brain activity through visual or aural feedback in a VR environment.

As these technologies continue to progress, we may see more tailored and adaptable VR experiences for emotional management. These could employ AI to alter the virtual environment and obstacles based on the user's real-time emotional state and progress over time. For those with ADHD, this might entail highly individualized emotional regulation training that evolves with their needs and talents.

It's crucial to emphasize that while VR and biofeedback applications offer exciting potential for emotional management, they should be utilized as part of a holistic therapy approach, ideally under the guidance of a mental health expert. The usefulness of these technologies might differ among individuals, and it's vital to verify that skills taught in virtual settings transition effectively to real-world circumstances.

Privacy and potential adverse effects, including motion sickness or eye strain from prolonged VR use, are also key factors. Users should be cautious of the amount of personal data captured by these applications and follow rules for the safe and pleasant use of VR technology.

In conclusion, Virtual Reality and biofeedback applications represent a frontier in emotional management technology, giving immersive, interactive, and individualized approaches to training emotional control skills. For individuals with ADHD, these technologies provide unique possibilities to practice emotional management skills in controlled yet realistic contexts, perhaps leading to increased emotional awareness and regulation in daily life.

Chapter Nine

Intersectionality and Neurodiversity in ADHD

Gender and ADHD: Emotional Regulation Differences

The interaction of gender and ADHD provides a complex picture, particularly when it comes to emotional control. Historically, ADHD has been disproportionately diagnosed in males, leading to a bias in the study and understanding of the disorder. However, new research has indicated that ADHD appears differently among genders, especially in terms of emotional regulation.

In females, ADHD generally presents with more internalizing symptoms, such as anxiety and depression, which can greatly influence emotional control. Women with ADHD may feel more intense emotions and struggle with mood swings, leading to issues in personal and professional relationships. They may also be more prone to rumination and negative self-talk, aggravating emotional dysregulation.

Males with ADHD, on the other hand, tend to exhibit more externalizing tendencies, such as violence or impulsivity. This might emerge as outbursts of rage or irritation, leading to difficulties in controlling emotional responses in social contexts. However, it's crucial to recognize that these are broad tendencies, and individual experiences may vary greatly.

Hormonal variations play a crucial influence in emotional control for both genders but can have a more pronounced effect on females with ADHD. The menstrual cycle, pregnancy, and menopause can all alter ADHD symptoms and mental stability.

For instance, many women report an exacerbation of ADHD symptoms and emotional volatility during the premenstrual phase.

Societal expectations and gender norms also influence how emotional dysregulation in ADHD is viewed and addressed. Women are generally expected to be more emotionally attuned and in charge, which can lead to greater stress and masking behaviors in people with ADHD. Men, however, may face stigma for expressing emotional vulnerability, perhaps leading to repression of emotions and poor coping techniques.

The way ADHD is diagnosed and treated also changes between genders. Girls and women are generally diagnosed later in life compared to boys and men, partly because their symptoms may be misattributed to other diseases or personality factors. This delayed diagnosis can result in years of neglected emotional regulation difficulties, potentially leading to more ingrained patterns of emotional dysregulation.

Treatment techniques for emotional regulation in ADHD may need to be customized based on gender. For example, women might benefit more from interventions that address internalized negative self-perceptions and anxiety, whereas men would require greater focus on impulse control and anger management tactics.

Healthcare providers need to be aware of these gender disparities in emotional control within ADHD. A more sophisticated knowledge can lead to more accurate diagnoses and more successful, individualized treatment regimens. This involves investigating how gender identity, rather than just biological sex, might alter the experience of ADHD and emotional regulation.

Research in this field is continuing, and our understanding of gender variations in ADHD and emotional control continues to evolve. Future studies that cover varied gender identities and expressions will be crucial in building a more thorough picture of how gender connects with ADHD and emotional regulation.

Ultimately, while gender can influence the presentation and experience of emotional dysregulation in ADHD, it's crucial to approach each individual's situation with an open mind, evaluating their unique experiences and needs beyond gender-based stereotypes.

ADHD in Different Cultural Contexts

Attention Deficit Hyperactivity Disorder (ADHD) is a neurodevelopmental disorder that affects individuals across the globe. However, its perception, diagnosis, and management might differ greatly depending on cultural circumstances.

Understanding these cultural variations is vital for delivering effective, culturally relevant assistance for individuals with ADHD.

In Western countries, notably in North America and Europe, ADHD is generally recognized and diagnosed. The medical model of ADHD is prominent, with a focus on symptom treatment through medication and behavioral interventions. However, even within Western societies, there are variances. For instance, in the United States, ADHD is more routinely diagnosed and medicated compared to European countries, where a more conservative approach to diagnosis and treatment is often used.

In contrast, many non-Western societies have traditionally been less likely to acknowledge ADHD as a unique disorder. In some Asian cultures, for example, behaviors associated with ADHD might be attributed to a lack of discipline or poor parenting rather than a neurological difference. This cultural perception might lead to stigma and a reluctance to seek professional care.

The concept of emotional control itself might vary between cultures. In individualistic societies, mainly found in Western countries, there's often an emphasis on personal emotional expression and self-regulation. Collectivist societies, more frequent in Asian and African cultures, may place greater value on emotional control and contemplate the impact of one's emotions on community harmony.

Cultural attitudes concerning hyperactivity and impulsivity, two essential components of ADHD, also differ. In some cultures, great energy and assertiveness could be appreciated attributes, while in others, tranquility and reflectiveness are highly prized. These cultural norms can influence whether ADHD-like behaviors are perceived as troublesome or within the range of normal variance.

The role of family in addressing ADHD also varies culturally. In many non-Western cultures, extended family plays a key part in child-rearing and may be more involved in managing a family member's ADHD. This can be both supporting and challenging, as it may give a strong support network but also raise the pressure to conform to cultural norms.

Educational systems and their approach to learning differences also impact how ADHD is understood and managed. Some school systems may be more flexible with varied learning styles and behaviors, while others may have tighter standards of compliance, perhaps making it more problematic for those with ADHD.

Traditional and alternative medical practices in different countries can also influence ADHD management. For instance, in some Asian cultures, traditional herbal medicines or methods like acupuncture could be sought out as therapies for

ADHD symptoms, either alongside or instead of Western medical approaches.

Language and communication patterns between countries can alter how ADHD symptoms are described and interpreted. The vocabulary used to express attention, hyperactivity, and impulsivity may not have direct equivalents in all languages, thereby altering how ADHD is perceived and communicated.

It's crucial to highlight that globalization is bringing some convergence in understanding ADHD across cultures. As knowledge becomes more readily available and cross-cultural exchanges rise, there's a rising understanding of ADHD as a neurodevelopmental condition in many parts of the world.

For healthcare providers and educators working with persons from varied cultural backgrounds, cultural competence is vital. This entails not just understanding diverse cultural viewpoints on ADHD but also being able to communicate successfully across cultural lines and adapt interventions to be culturally acceptable.

Research into ADHD across diverse cultural contexts is ongoing and crucial. More culturally diverse studies are needed to understand how ADHD presents in different communities and to develop culturally sensitive diagnostic tools and therapies. This research can assist in guaranteeing that persons with ADHD receive adequate support, regardless of their cultural background.

Embracing Neurodiversity While Managing Emotions

The concept of neurodiversity, which holds that neurological variances like ADHD are natural variations in human neurocognition rather than diseases to be remedied, has gained substantial support in recent years. This paradigm shift offers a new view on ADHD, stressing strengths with obstacles. However, it also raises challenges about how to reconcile recognizing neurodiversity with the need to manage the frequently painful emotional experiences associated with ADHD.

At its foundation, the neurodiversity movement wants society to regard ADHD and other neurodevelopmental problems as part of the spectrum of human diversity, just like we view distinctions in ethnicity or gender. This perspective can be motivating for those with ADHD, boosting self-acceptance and minimizing stigma. It admits that ADHD brains are simply wired differently, not deficiently.

However, embracing neurodiversity doesn't imply disregarding the genuine issues that come with ADHD, particularly in the field of emotional regulation. Many individuals with ADHD struggle with high emotions, mood swings, and trouble managing irritation or rage. These emotional issues can greatly impair the quality of life, relationships, and overall well-being.

The answer lies in finding a balance between praising the particular talents of the ADHD brain while also creating techniques to handle its more troublesome elements. This balanced approach emphasizes that while ADHD is a natural variety, the culture we live in is frequently not built to support neurodivergent individuals, needing some level of adaptation.

One way to embrace this balance is to reframe emotional regulation tactics not as ways to "fix" the ADHD brain, but as tools to help it function optimally in a neurotypical world. For example, mindfulness techniques can be presented not as a strategy to modify the ADHD brain, but as a means to harness its natural tendencies towards intense focus and heightened awareness.

It's also crucial to note that many emotional control practices can assist everyone, regardless of neurocognitive state. Practices like detecting and labeling emotions, employing coping strategies for stress, and strengthening communication skills are useful life skills for all persons. Framing these tactics as universal tools rather than ADHD-specific interventions can help preserve a neurodiversity-affirming attitude.

The neurodiversity perspective can boost emotional control attempts by fostering self-compassion. Understanding that one's emotional experiences are part of their unique brain makeup can lessen self-blame and shame, which typically increase emotional dysregulation. This self-compassion can establish a more positive basis for developing emotional management abilities.

Education plays a critical role in balancing neurodiversity and emotional control. Teaching persons with ADHD, their families, and the broader society about both the strengths and challenges associated with ADHD helps develop understanding and support. This teaching should emphasize that getting treatment for emotional regulation is not in conflict with accepting neurodiversity, but rather a manner of acknowledging one's unique needs.

In professional settings, the neurodiversity paradigm might inform how accommodations are approached. Instead of focusing exclusively on alleviating weaknesses, accommodations might be viewed as approaches to optimize the work environment for diverse neurological patterns. This can include offering quiet rooms for emotional management, allowing flexible work hours to support ADHD-related sleep patterns, or utilizing hyperfocus inclinations in project planning.

It's also crucial to consider how embracing neurodiversity overlaps with mental health. While

ADHD alone is not a mental illness, it often co-occurs with conditions like anxiety and depression. A balanced approach emphasizes that while ADHD is a natural variance, concomitant mental health disorders may require specific attention.

The function of medicine in ADHD management might be a challenging topic within the neurodiversity paradigm. While some perceive medication as at odds with recognizing natural neurological variances, others see it as a tool that helps them to more fully express their real selves. A balanced approach sees medicine as a personal choice that can be part of embracing one's neurodivergent identity if it promotes quality of life.

Ultimately, recognizing neurodiversity while regulating emotions in ADHD is about finding a personalized balance. It involves enjoying the unique aspects of the ADHD brain while simultaneously acknowledging and resolving its limitations. This balanced approach can lead to a more positive self-image, greater emotional control, and a life that acknowledges both the strengths and needs of the neurodivergent individual.

Chapter Ten

Long-Term Strategies and Advocacy

Developing a Personalized Emotional Regulation Toolkit

Creating a tailored emotional regulation toolset is a vital step in the long-term management of ADHD-related emotional problems. This toolbox should be a collection of ideas, techniques, and resources adapted to an individual's personal needs, interests, and lifestyle. The process of establishing this toolbox is ongoing and grows as the individual acquires more insight into their emotional patterns and discovers what works best for them.

The first step in designing a tailored toolset is self-assessment. This involves identifying unique emotional control difficulties, recognizing triggers, and understanding personal emotional patterns. Keeping an emotion journal can be beneficial in this process, allowing individuals to chronicle their emotional experiences over time and spot repeating themes or situations that lead to emotional dysregulation.

Once these patterns are found, the next stage is to research and experiment with various emotional management tactics. These could include cognitive-behavioral approaches, mindfulness practices, physical activities, artistic outlets, or technology help. It's crucial to explore a wide range of tactics, as what works for one individual may not work for another.

Cognitive-behavioral therapies could include tactics like cognitive restructuring (challenging and reframing negative thoughts), problem-solving skills, and stress inoculation training. These approaches assist individuals shift cognitive processes that contribute to emotional dysregulation.

Mindfulness methods, such as meditation, deep breathing exercises, or body scans, can be helpful aids for emotional management. These activities help individuals become more aware of their emotional states and respond to them more effectively rather than reacting impulsively.

Physical tactics are often underestimated yet can be incredibly effective. Regular exercise, yoga, or even simple things like taking a stroll can have a big impact on emotional mood. For some individuals with ADHD, physical activity can be a significant component of emotional regulation.

Creative endeavors such as art, music, writing, or dancing can give a form of emotional expression and regulation. These hobbies can serve as both a tool to process emotions and a calming influence during times of emotional instability.

Technological assistance can also be a valuable component of an emotional control toolset. This can involve apps for mood tracking, guided meditation, or cognitive-behavioral activities. Wearable devices that measure physiological indications of stress can also be helpful for some individuals.

It's crucial to include both proactive and reactive methods in the toolkit. Proactive methods are used routinely to preserve emotional balance and prevent dysregulation, while reactive tactics are applied at the moment when confronting emotional issues.

The toolset should also contain environmental adjustments. This can mean creating a relaxing environment at home or work, employing noise-canceling headphones to handle sensory overload, or adopting routines that encourage emotional stability.

Social support is another key piece of the emotional control toolset. This can include selecting specific friends or family members to seek out during emotional issues, joining support groups, or engaging with a therapist or coach.

As the toolkit is built, it's crucial to describe what works and what doesn't. This can be done through journaling, using a spreadsheet, or developing a visual representation like a mind map. The paperwork should be easily available, potentially in a digital format that can be retrieved from a smartphone.

Regular assessment and refinement of the toolbox are vital. As life circumstances change and individuals grow in their awareness of their ADHD and emotional patterns, the toolbox should be modified accordingly. This might require introducing new techniques, changing old ones, or deleting those that are no longer effective.

Ultimately, a well-developed emotional regulation toolkit delivers a sense of empowerment and control. It gives persons with ADHD realistic skills to manage their emotions successfully, leading to greater quality of life and better overall functioning. The process of establishing and improving this toolkit is a journey of self-discovery and growth, contributing to long-term success in managing ADHD-related emotional difficulties.

Maintaining Progress and Preventing Relapse

Maintaining improvement in emotional regulation and preventing relapse is an important element of long-term ADHD care. While developing strategies and techniques is necessary, continuously applying them over time and adapting to new difficulties is also important. This process demands continual work, self-awareness, and the ability to alter one's approach as circumstances change.

One crucial element in continuing success is the formation of a routine that integrates emotional management activities. This can include daily mindfulness exercises, regular check-ins with a therapist or support group, or allocated time for stress-reducing activities. Consistency is key, as consistent practice helps consolidate these methods as habits, making them more natural and easier to adopt during hard circumstances.

However, it's crucial to remember that advancement is not necessarily linear. Individuals with ADHD may endure setbacks or periods where emotional management becomes more problematic. These changes are normal and should be considered as chances for learning and growth rather than failures. Developing a growth mindset, where setbacks are regarded as opportunities to progress rather than insurmountable hurdles, can help retain drive and resilience.

Regular self-assessment is vital for maintaining development. This could involve frequently examining emotional journals, reflecting on recent events, or utilizing standardized testing instruments to measure changes in emotional regulation skills over time. These assessments can assist in identifying areas of improvement as well as areas that may need further focus.

It's also crucial to be proactive in recognizing potential triggers or situations that can contribute to emotional dysregulation. This could involve big life changes, increasing stress at work, or changes in relationships. By anticipating these problems, individuals can prepare by reinforcing their emotional management techniques or seeking additional support when needed.

Preventing relapse also entails continual education about ADHD and emotional regulation. Staying educated about new research, treatment options, and tactics can bring fresh views and tools to add to one's emotional regulation toolkit. This could involve reading books or articles, attending workshops or conferences, or participating in online groups dedicated to ADHD.

Building a strong support network is vital for maintaining progress and preventing relapse. This network could include family members, friends, mental health experts, and peers with ADHD. Regular communication with this support network can provide encouragement, accountability, and aid during hard times.

It's also crucial to recognize victories, no matter how minor. Recognizing and acknowledging progress can enhance motivation and encourage beneficial actions. This can involve keeping a "success journal" or sharing achievements with a support network.

Flexibility is crucial in maintaining long-term progress. As life circumstances change, once effective techniques may need to be altered or replaced. Being open to testing new ways and altering existing strategies can assist in ensuring continuing success in emotional regulation.

Self-care has a critical role in maintaining development and preventing relapse. This includes things like getting appropriate sleep, maintaining a good diet, and regular exercise, as well as activities that promote relaxation and stress reduction. Neglecting self-care can lead to increased sensitivity to emotional dysregulation.

For many individuals with ADHD, medication plays a role in treating symptoms, including emotional regulation. Regular check-ins with healthcare providers to monitor the effectiveness of medicine and make modifications as needed can be a crucial element of maintaining improvement.

Technology can be exploited to assist continual advancement. This may involve using applications to track mood and emotional regulation attempts, creating reminders for self-care tasks, or employing wearable technology to monitor physiological indications of stress.

It's also crucial to have a plan in place for handling setbacks. This can include a list of emergency coping skills, contact information for support folks, or a step-by-step approach to achieving emotional equilibrium. Having this strategy readily available can provide a sense of stability and a clear route forward during hard circumstances.

Ultimately, maintaining improvement and preventing relapse in emotional regulation is a continual process that involves commitment, self-awareness, and adaptation. By regularly using methods, being informed, maintaining a strong support network, and remaining adaptable in the face of change, individuals with ADHD can achieve long-term success in regulating their emotional well-being.

Self-Advocacy and Educating Others about ADHD and Emotions

Self-advocacy and teaching others about ADHD and its emotional implications are key components of managing the condition effectively and establishing a more understanding and supportive environment. For many adults with ADHD, learning to advocate for themselves and educate others is a path that needs courage, knowledge, and effective communication skills.

Self-advocacy begins with a solid understanding of one's own ADHD and its impact on emotional regulation. This requires not only recognizing obstacles but also finding strengths and special features connected with ADHD. By gaining this self-awareness, individuals can better explain their needs and experiences to others.

Education is a vital part of self-advocacy. This includes remaining updated on the current research on ADHD and emotional regulation, recognizing one's rights in various settings (such as the workplace or educational institutions), and being aware of available services and accommodations. This understanding helps individuals to speak boldly about their situation and seek appropriate support.

One crucial component of self-advocacy is learning to communicate effectively about ADHD and emotional management. This requires being able to define ADHD in clear, accessible terms, outlining how it affects daily living, and identifying specific needs or accommodations. It's important to construct a "personal impact statement" that summarizes how ADHD impacts one's emotions and actions.

In the workplace, self-advocacy could involve discussing ADHD with employers or HR departments to request acceptable accommodations. This could involve discussing how specific environmental conditions affect emotional regulation and providing remedies, such as a calmer workstation or flexible deadlines.

In personal relationships, self-advocacy requires open conversation with partners, family members, and friends regarding ADHD-related emotional issues. This could include educating loved ones about emotional dysregulation, reviewing triggers, and explaining how they can provide support during stressful times.

Educating others about ADHD and emotions extends beyond personal circles. Many adults with

ADHD find it enjoyable to join in broader advocacy campaigns. This can be engaging in ADHD support groups, speaking at community events, publishing blogs or articles, or sharing experiences on social media platforms.

When teaching people, it's crucial to address common misconceptions regarding ADHD, particularly those connected to the emotional elements of the disorder. Many individuals are unaware that emotional dysregulation is a basic component of ADHD, frequently equating the disease simply with concentration and hyperactivity concerns.

Sharing personal tales can be a valuable tool in educating others. By offering specific instances of how ADHD affects emotional experiences, individuals can help others build empathy and understanding. However, it's crucial to create boundaries and discuss just what feels comfortable.

It's also vital to educate others on the range of ADHD experiences. This includes showing how ADHD can appear differently across genders, ethnicities, and age groups, particularly in terms of emotional regulation.

In educational contexts, self-advocacy could involve working with teachers or administrators to develop accommodations that help emotional regulation. This could include alternatives for taking breaks during class, alternate testing environments, or extended time for homework.

Technology can be a significant tool in self-advocacy and education activities. Social media platforms, blogs, and online forums allow possibilities to share information and personal experiences with a wide audience. Additionally, there are several apps and online resources that may be shared to assist others in understanding and supporting those with ADHD.

When educating others about ADHD and emotions, it's crucial to underline that while ADHD provides obstacles, it also comes with unique capabilities. This balanced approach can assist reduce stigma and encourage a more sophisticated understanding of neurodiversity.

Self-advocacy also requires understanding when and how to seek professional support. This can include working with a therapist who specializes in ADHD, meeting with an ADHD coach, or attending support groups. Being able to express one's demands to healthcare practitioners is a crucial part of self-advocacy.

Lastly, it's crucial to remember that self-advocacy and education are continual activities. As understanding of ADHD evolves and personal experiences vary, the strategy for self-advocacy may need to be altered. Remaining open to learning and adjusting one's advocacy techniques is crucial to long-term success.

By effectively advocating for themselves and teaching others about ADHD and its emotional aspects, individuals can create more supportive environments, eliminate stigma, and enhance the overall quality of life for themselves and those impacted by ADHD.

Made in United States
Troutdale, OR
12/27/2024

27309384R00106